Cambridge Little Steps 3

Second Edition

Activity Book

Gabriela Zapiain

Contents

1. What do we do at school?   3
2. How do we feel?   17
3. How are we the same and different?   31
4. What is a wild animal?   45
5. Who helps our community?   59
6. What do we do in restaurants?   73
7. What is a routine?   87
8. How can we care for the Earth?   101
9. What do we do on vacation?   115

Picture Dictionary   129

Stickers

What do we do at school?

 Stick. Draw. Say. Trace.

Monday	Tuesday	Wednesday	Thursday

Friday	Saturday	Sunday

Vocabulary: *Monday, Tuesday, Wednesday, Thursday, Friday, Saturday, Sunday.* Point to and say each new word. Children repeat after you. Point to the first sticker. Say: *School. When do you go to school?* Point to Monday and encourage children to say the day. Say: *Stick the school.* Children stick the sticker on Monday. Repeat with *Sunday* and *park.* Then point to Tuesday and ask children to draw something they do on that day. They could draw themselves doing an activity, or draw an object to represent the activity. Repeat with the other days (Wednesday–Saturday). Then children point to each day and say: *On (Thursday), I (paint).* Finally, children trace the words.

Unit 1 3

⭕ Circle. 😊 Say.   Story

Monday	Thursday	Thursday	Friday
Friday	Tuesday and Wednesday	Monday	Tuesday and Wednesday

Unit 1

Language: *What day is this in the story? On (Monday), we learn (to be tidy and neat).* Ask children to remember the story. Children look at the first scene from the story. Point to the two days under it and read them aloud. Children repeat. Ask: *What day is this in the story?* Children circle the correct day. *(Monday.)* Repeat with the other scenes. Children then retell the story, using the scenes for reference.

 Say. Match. Trace.

Phonics

trees

wings

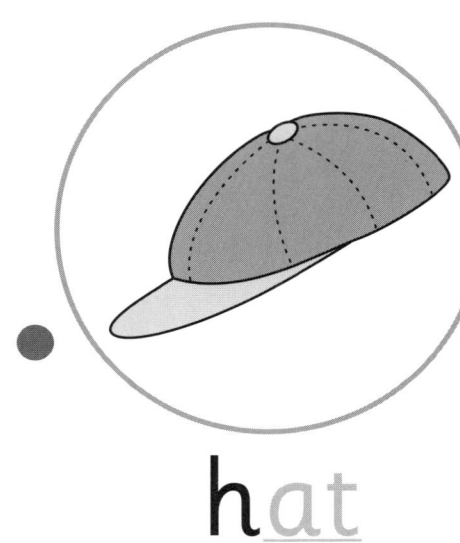

hat

things

bees

Phonics: *bees, trees; things, wings* (rhyming words). Point to each picture and say the word. Children repeat. Point to the trees, and say the word, emphasizing the "ee" sound. Say: *What sounds like trees? (Bees.)* Repeat with *wings* and *things*. Then point to the hat and say the word, emphasizing the "a" sound. Say: *Is there a word that sounds like hat? (No.)* Children draw lines to match the pairs of rhyming words. Finally, children trace the letters that make the rhyming sounds, saying the words as they do so.

Unit 1 5

 Say. ✓ Mark. 🖍 Color.

Literacy

Do you like the story?

Literacy: Identifying details from a story. Point to the first picture. Ask: *Is this from the story? (Yes.) What happens?* Elicit what children remember about this picture in the story. They put a check mark in the box next to the picture. Repeat with the other pictures. Children put a check mark next to the pictures that are from the story. For those that are not from the story, ask children what detail is different (in the second picture the boy isn't playing soccer, and in the fourth picture the boy isn't singing; he's using a computer). Finally, ask: *Do you like the story?* Children color the face that shows their opinion of the story.

 Look. Say. Color.

Values

Values: Helping others at school. Point to the boy helping the teacher. Ask: *What is he doing? Is he helping? (Yes.) Who is he helping?* Then point to the girl at the table who is not helping (she isn't sharing or passing the crayons). Repeat and discuss what she could do better. Finally, children identify and color the children who are helping.

Unit 1 7

😀 Say. ⭐ Match. ✏️ Trace. 🖍️ Color.

Vocabulary

Art •

Math •

Science •

Physical Education •

Writing •

Reading •

Vocabulary: *Science, Art, Math, Writing, Reading, Physical Education.* Point to each picture on the right and have children name the school subject. Then, point to the first word on the left and say: *Art.* Children repeat after you. They draw a line to match the word to the correct picture. Repeat with the other words. Finally, children trace the words then choose their favorite subject and color that picture.

Look. Follow. Say. — Language

Monday
Tuesday
Wednesday
Thursday
Friday

Language: *What day is today? (Monday.) What do we have on (Monday)? We have (Art).* Children point to the pictures on the right and name the school subjects. Read the days of the week on the left, pointing to each day as you say it and encouraging children to repeat. Point to *Monday*. Ask: *What day is today? (Monday.) What do we have on Monday?* Children follow the path from Monday to Art, and answer: *We have Art!* They draw the line through the maze from Monday to Art. Children work through the other days and subjects in pairs, taking turns to ask and answer the questions.

 Say. Look. Color.

Concept

1 black
2 brown
3 red
4 orange
5 yellow
6 green
7 blue
8 purple
9 pink
10 gray

Concept: Recognizing colors. Point to the key on the left of the page. Point to each color word and read it together, with children repeating the word aloud. After repeating each word, children color the paint blob in the correct color to make a key. They then use their key to color the picture on the right. As they work, they talk about the colors they are using.

 Say. Trace. Write.

Vocabulary

1. play music

2. use a computer

3. paint with watercolors

4. speak English

5. read books

6. play in the playground

Vocabulary: *use a computer, play music, speak English, paint with watercolors, read books, play in the playground.* Point to each picture and have children name and mime the action. Repeat several times. Point to the first phrase and say: *One. Play music.* Children repeat and trace the words. Say it again and have children find the corresponding picture and write the number 1 in the box. Repeat with the other phrases.

Unit 1 · 11

👁 Look. 👄 Say. ✏ Draw.

Language

1   and  at  .

2   and  at  .

3  and  at  .

Language: *What does he / she do at school? He / She (plays in the playground).* Point to the first sentence and ask: *What does Leo do at school?* Point to each picture and read the sentence together: *He uses a computer and plays music at school.* Repeat with Mia. Then children draw a friend and two different activities the friend does at school. Ask volunteers to share their drawings and say what their friend does at school.

Look. Match. Say.

Speaking

"I need a chair, please."

"Here you go."

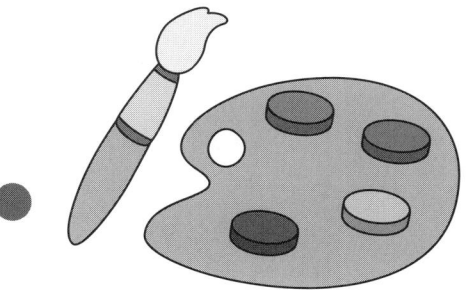

 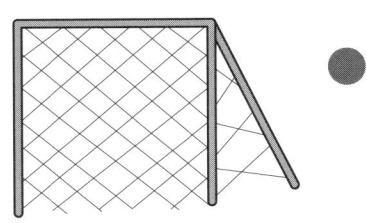

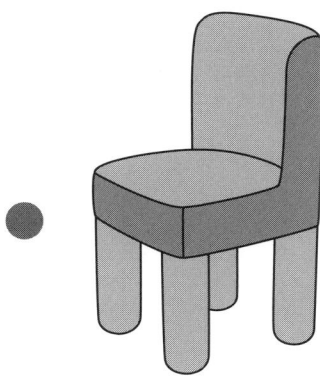

Language: *I need a (chair), please. Here you go. Thank you. What does she / he need? She / He needs (a chair).* Point to the top picture of Mia and ask: *What does she need? (She needs a chair.)* Children draw lines to match the characters on the left to the things they need on the right. Then focus on Mia again, and read the speech bubbles. Children repeat after you. Encourage a volunteer to mime giving you a chair as they say: *Here you go.* Say: *Thank you.* Invite children to the front to act out the three role-plays on the page. Children can then practice acting them out in pairs.

Unit 1 13

Trace. Draw. Color. Say.

Cross-curricular: Art

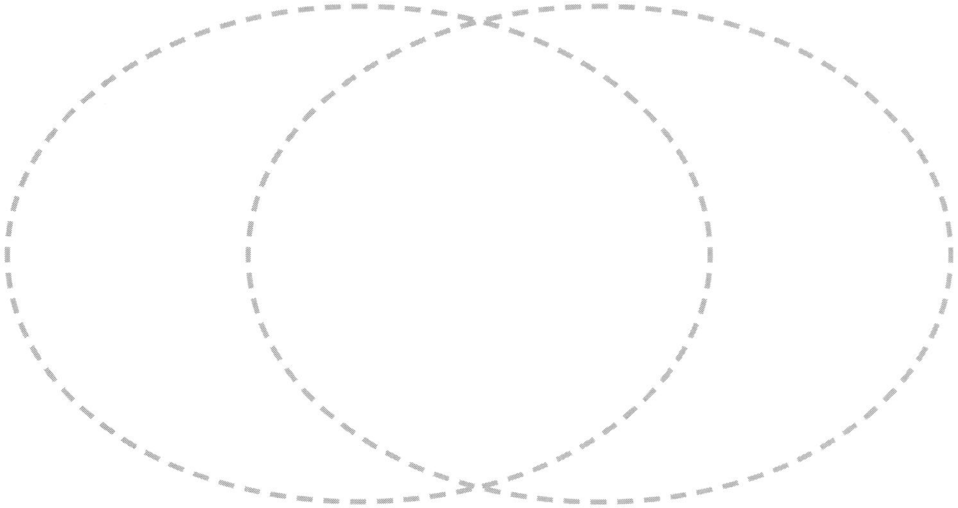

yellow   red   yellow   blue

orange   green

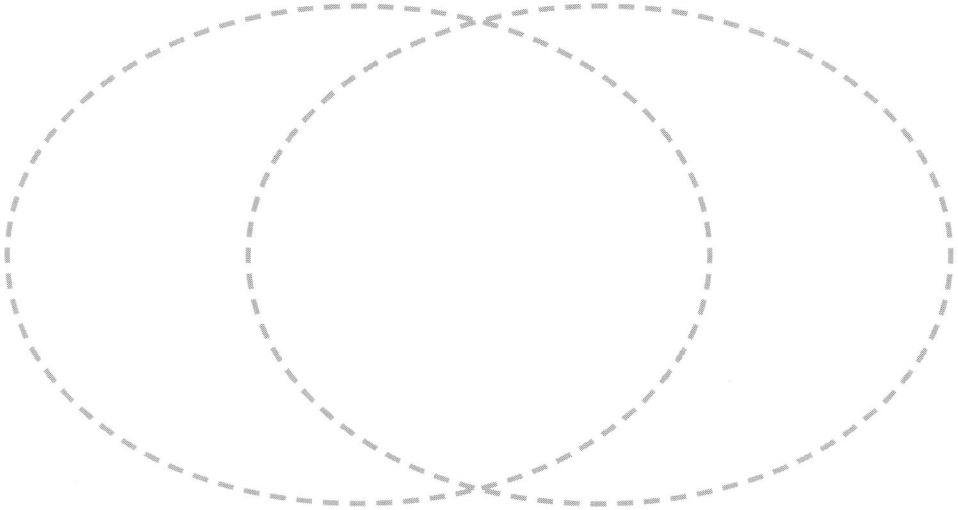

blue   red

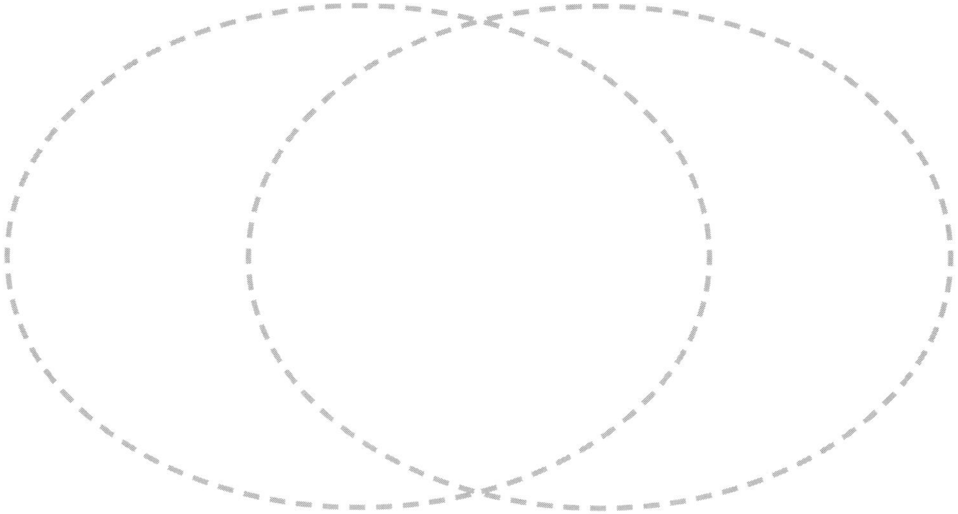

purple

Art: Making secondary colors. Point to the first diagram. Point to and read the word *yellow*. Children repeat after you. Ask children to trace the left-hand circle in yellow. Repeat with the red circle. Then point to the central space in the diagram and say: *Yellow and red make …? (Orange.)* Point to the word label as you say the word. Children draw and color something orange in the space. Repeat with the other diagrams. Finally, children describe their drawings to one another: *It's a (carrot). It's (orange).*

Look.  Count. Trace.

Numeracy

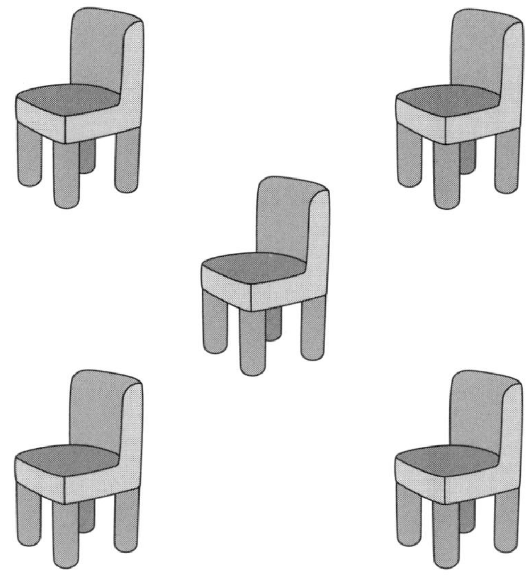

5
10

10
20

15
20

5
15

Numeracy: *five, ten, fifteen, twenty*. Point to the chairs. Ask: *How many chairs? Let's count.* Children count the chairs. They then trace the correct number. Repeat with the other pictures.

 Say. Circle. Draw. Color.

Review

What do we do at school?

My favorite word in Unit 1 is:

Unit 1

Vocabulary and Language Review: Ask the Big Question: *What do we do at school?* Children look back through Unit 1 to recall what they have learned. Ask children to look at the 10 pictures from Unit 1. They say the words then circle the pictures that they are able to name. Accept all possible answers. Then ask: *What is your favorite word in this unit?* Remind children of the words from the vocabulary lessons. Children draw a picture of their favorite word. They then present their pictures to the class saying: *My favorite word is ...* . Answer the Big Question together, using their drawings and the pictures on the left as prompts. Finally, focus on the self-assessment activity. Ask: *How did you do in this unit?* Children color the face that shows how they feel they did.

2 How do we feel?

● Stick. ➡ Follow. ◡ Say. ✏ Trace.

Vocabulary: *scared, excited, surprised, bored, shy, silly*. Point to each picture and say the word. Children point to the pictures and repeat after you. Say: *(Excited / Surprised)*. Stick *(excited / surprised)*. Children stick each sticker as you say it. Then point to the first word on the top left and say: *Scared*. Children repeat, follow the path through the maze, and draw a line to match the word with the correct picture. Repeat with the other words. They can use a different color for each line. They then point to each word, mime the feeling, and say the word. Finally, children trace the words. Children can color the faces in colors of their preference.

Unit 2 17

◯ Circle. ◡ Say.

Story

1 2 3 4

1 2 3 4

1 2 3 4

1 2 3 4

Language: *Is this picture (first) in the story? Which picture is (first)? At first, Maddy is scared. Then, she is excited.* Look at the scenes from the story. Point to the first scene and ask: *Is this picture first in the story? (No.)* Ask: *Which picture is first?* Children point to the correct scene. They circle the number 1 under the scene to show that it is the first. Repeat with the second, third, and last scenes. Children then retell the story, using the scenes for reference.

 Say. Circle. Trace.

Phonics

cake

bee

bake

things

wait

train

Phonics: *bake, cake, wait* /eɪ/. Point to each picture in the first row and say the word. Children repeat. Point to the cake and say the word, emphasizing the /eɪ/ sound. Say: /eɪ/, *cake. Same sound? (Yes.)* Repeat with *bee (No.)* and *bake (Yes.)* Children circle the pictures with the /eɪ/ sound. Repeat with the second row. Finally, children trace the letters that make the /eɪ/ sound, saying the words as they do so.

😀 Say. ✓ Mark. ✏ Color.

Literacy

scared ☐

sad ☐

excited ☐

silly ☐

bored ☐

happy ☐

shy ☐

Do you like the story? 🙂 😐 ☹

Literacy: Identifying how characters feel in a story. Ask children to think about the story and remember how Maddy feels. Point to the *excited* picture. Ask: *How does she feel? (Excited.) Does Maddy feel like this in the story? (Yes.) When? Why?* Elicit what children remember about this in the story. They put a check mark in the box next to the word *excited*. Repeat with the other pictures. Children put a check mark next to those feelings that Maddy has in the story. Finally, ask: *Do you like the story?* Children color the face that shows their opinion of the story.

👁 **Look.** ✦ **Match.** ◡ **Say.**

Values

Values: Talking about your feelings. Point to the boy on the top left and ask: *How does he feel? Why?* Then ask: *Who does he talk to about his feelings? (A friend.)* Children trace the line and point to the correct picture. Ask: *How does he feel now? Why?* Children find and point to the third picture of the sequence. They then draw a line to match the second and the third pictures of the sequence. Repeat with the pictures of the girls.

Unit 2 21

 Say. Trace. Write.

Vocabulary

1. scream

2. shout hooray

3. jump up and down

4. yawn

5. cry

6. laugh

Vocabulary: *scream, jump up and down, cry, yawn, shout hooray, laugh.* Point to each picture and have children name and mime the action. Repeat several times. Point to the first word and say: *One. Scream.* Children repeat and trace the word. Say it again and have children find the corresponding picture and write the number 1 in the box. Repeat with the other words.

 **Think. Draw. Say.** **Language**

1. When I'm  I _____ .

2. When I'm  I _____ .

3. When I'm  I _____ .

Language: *What do you do when you're (bored)? When I'm (bored), I (yawn).* Point to the first part of the first sentence and read it together: *When I'm sad, ...* Elicit from children what they do when they're sad: *I (cry).* Accept all children's ideas. Encourage children to draw a face of someone crying (or something else, depending on their answer). Repeat with the other sentences. Finally, encourage children to read their sentences aloud. Optional: Children can color the faces according to their preference.

 Look. Say. Draw.

Concept

Concept: Completing a pattern. Children point to and name each feeling. Then, they look at the pattern in each row and say what feeling should come next. Guide them through the first row. Say: *happy, sad, happy, sad, happy ... What comes next? (Sad.)* Children draw a sad face in the empty space. Continue with the other rows. In the last row, children can invent and draw their own pattern. Once children have finished drawing, ask them to say the words in the completed patterns.

¹²³ Count.   ✓ Color.   a✎ Write.   ◯ Trace.

Vocabulary

candy   cake   candle   balloon   present   party hat

Vocabulary: *candy, cake, candle, balloon, present, party hat*. Children point to and name each party item at the top of the page. Point to the candy and ask: *How many candies?* Then point to the larger picture and ask children to count how many candies they can find. Children find all the candies and color them in the same color. They then count and answer: *Four! Four candies*, and write the number in the box. Repeat with the other items. Finally, children trace the words.

Unit 2

Think. Draw. Color. Say.

Language

Language: *How many (balloons) are there? There are (six). What color are the (candles)? They're (blue).* Explain that the picture is incomplete, and that children will complete it. Say: *Look at the cake. Draw candles on the cake.* Children draw and color candles. Make sure they understand that they can choose how many to draw, and what color they are. Repeat with presents on the table, and balloons on the floor. When they finish, invite a volunteer to the front and ask: *How many (candles) are there in your picture? What color are the (candles)?* Repeat several times with other children. Children can work in pairs, taking turns to ask and answer the questions about their pictures.

 Think.  Say. Point. Color.

Speaking

Language: *How old are you? I'm (five) years old.* Point to the first picture and count the candles on the cake with the children. Then read the speech bubbles aloud. Children point and repeat after you. Count the candles on all the cakes with the children. Ask children to choose one child from the page. Invite a child to the front and have the class ask: *How old are you?* The child answers as if they were their chosen child from the page: *I'm (six) years old.* Children point to the correct child in their book. Children work in pairs or groups, taking turns to ask and answer the question with different answers. Finally, children color the picture of the child on the page whose age is the same as their own.

Unit 2   27

 Look. Say. Color.

Cross-curricular: Art

Art: Using art to express our feelings. Point to the children singing. Ask: *What are they doing? Are they using art to express their feelings?* (Yes.) Then point to the girl reading a book and ask: *What is she doing? Is she using art to express her feelings?* (No.) Finally, children identify and color the children who are expressing their feelings through art.

 Count. Match. Trace.

Numeracy

20

30

Numeracy: *thirty*. Point to the presents and ask: *How many presents can you see?* Count the presents in the first row (10), then say: *Let's count by tens.* Children count and answer, then match the group to the correct number and trace the number. Repeat with the balloons. Finally, they count by tens to 30.

Unit 2 29

 Say. Circle. Draw. Color.

Review

How do we feel?

My favorite word in Unit 2 is:

Unit 2

3 How are we the same and different?

 Stick.  Match.   Say.   Trace.

child     men

woman     women

 man    children

Vocabulary: *child, children, woman, women, man, men.* Point to the picture of a child and say the word. Children repeat. Then say: *Children.* Children point to the correct picture and repeat the word. Repeat with the other words. Say: *(Child / Children). Stick the (child / children).* Children stick each sticker as you say it. Say *One child. Three …? (Children.) One (woman). Three …? (Women.)* Children draw lines to match each word to its plural. In pairs, children practice, saying: *One (man). Three …? (Men.)* Finally, children trace the words. Children can color the people in colors of their preference.

Unit 3 31

 **Look. Draw. Say.**

Story

Unit 3

Language: *Is this picture correct? Why not? Joana is / isn't wearing glasses.* Look at the first scene from the story. Ask: *Is this correct?* (No.) *Why not?* (*Joana is wearing glasses in this scene in the story.*) Point to the glasses in the middle, and children draw Joana's glasses on the scene. Repeat with the other scenes, with children drawing the glasses where necessary. Children then retell the story, using the scenes for reference.

Say. Color. Trace.

Phonics

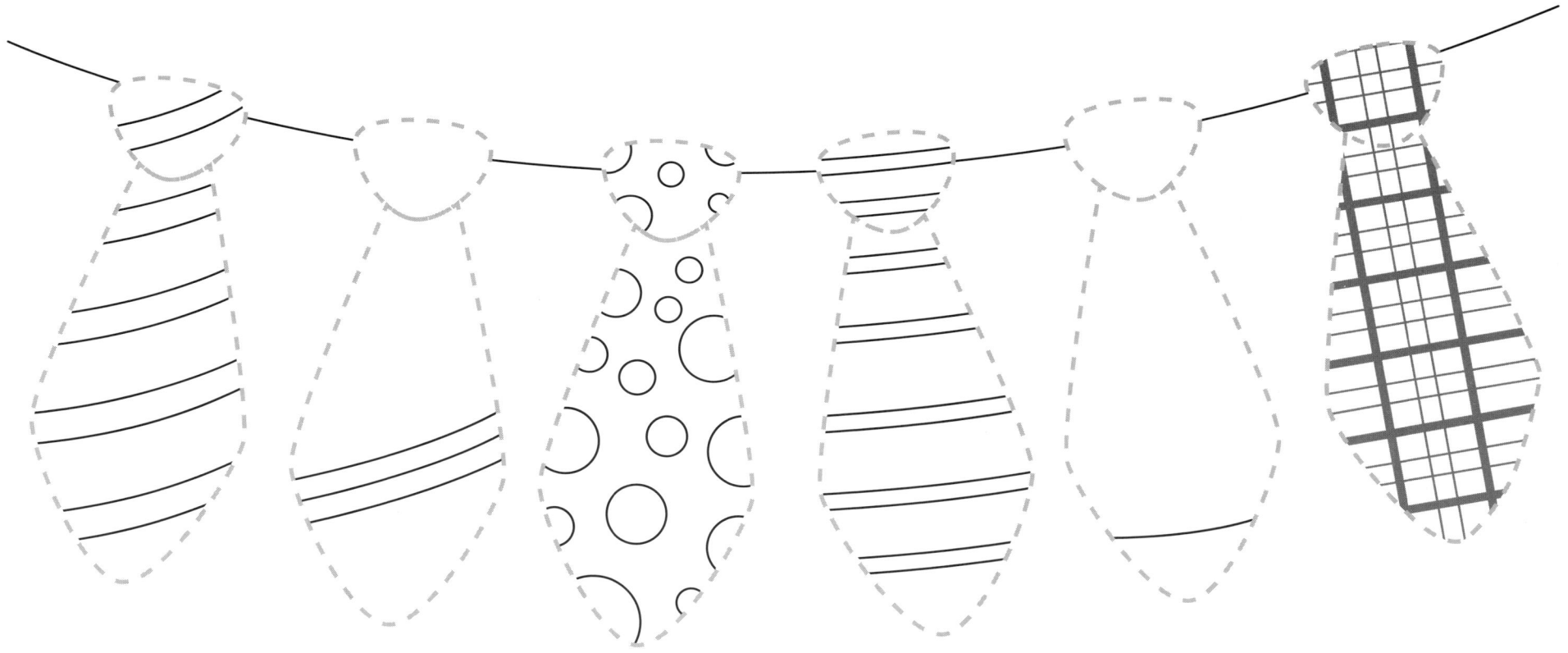

Five ties in a line.

 Say. ✓ Mark. ✏ Color.

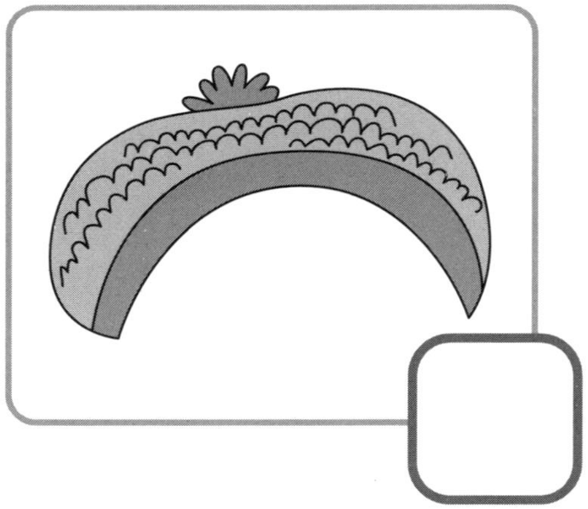

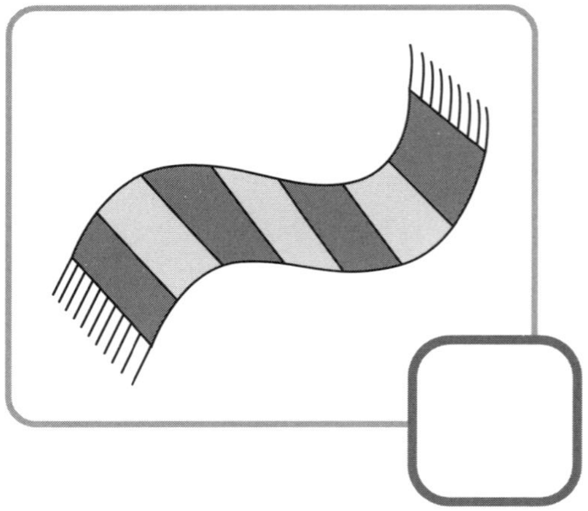

Literacy

Do you like the story? 😊 😐 ☹

Literacy: Identifying details from a story. Point to the first picture. Ask: *Is she from the story? (Yes.) Who is she? (Joana's mom.)* Elicit what children remember about this picture in the story. They put a check mark in the box next to the picture. Repeat with the other pictures. Children put a check mark next to those that are in the story (they shouldn't put a check mark next to the pictures of the man and the scarf). Finally, ask: *Do you like the story?* Children color the face that shows their opinion of the story.

✏️ Write. ✏️ Draw. 👄 Say.

Values

"I am proud of myself!"

Values: Being proud of yourself. Ask children: *Are you proud of yourself? Why?* Accept all their ideas and be encouraging. Point out that we can be proud of things we can do, things we have done, or things we are. Encourage all the children to think of something they're proud of. Point to the picture. Children write their name on the certificate, draw themselves doing something they're proud of, and decorate the child to look like them. Point to the speech bubble and read it aloud. Children repeat. Encourage children to present and describe their work to a partner or to the class.

 **Match. Say. Trace.**

Vocabulary

cousin

aunt

tall

uncle

short

Vocabulary: short, tall, aunt, cousin, uncle. Point to each word and read it aloud. Children point to and repeat the words. Point to the first word and say: *Uncle*. Ask: *Where's the uncle?* Children point to the uncle. They draw a line to match the word to the correct picture. Repeat with *aunt* and *cousin*. Then point to *tall*. Ask: *Who's tall?* Children match the word to the aunt and the uncle. Repeat with *short*. Children match the word to the cousin. Finally, children trace the words. Optional: Point to the (uncle) and ask: *Do you have (an uncle)?* Children circle the people they have in their family.

Unit 3

 Draw. Say.

Language

Language: *Who is she / he? She's / He's my (aunt). She's / He's a (woman). What does she / he look like? She's / He's (tall).* Children draw an aunt, uncle, cousin, or other person. Then, they present their drawings to the class and describe the family member, e.g., *This is my cousin. She's a child. She's a girl. She's short.* Encourage children to use prior knowledge to find other words to describe their family members, e.g., *She has long brown hair and green eyes. She's young.*

 **Look.** **Color.** **Say.** **Circle.**

Concept

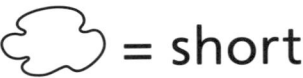 = short ⬜ = shorter ⬜ = the shortest

Say. Draw. Trace.

Vocabulary

short

red

straight

long

blond

curly

Vocabulary: *blond, red, long, short, curly, straight.* Point to the first picture of a child and read the word aloud. Children repeat. Then, they draw and color the corresponding hair on the picture. Repeat with the other words. Finally, children trace the words.

Unit 3　39

 Draw. Color. Talk.

Language

Language: *He / She has (curly black) hair. Who is it?* Point to the pictures on the left, and elicit the words *long, short, curly, straight*. Children look at the children in the top row of the page, and draw hair on them. They can choose the style and color of the hair. Invite a child to describe the hair they've drawn on boy 1: *He has (short black) hair.* Draw the hair on boy 1 in the bottom row in your book, and show children. Children work in pairs. They take turns to describe their pictures in the top row to their partner and to draw what their partner describes on the pictures in the bottom row.

 **Talk. Draw. Say.**

Speaking

Language: *What's your name? My name is (Leo). What's your favorite color? My favorite color is (green). His / Her name is (Leo). His / Her favorite color is (green).* Point to Mia and Leo, and read the speech bubbles next to them. Children repeat. Select a confident child and ask: *What's your name?* and then: *What's your favorite color?* Once they have responded, draw a simple picture of that child wearing clothes in their favorite color. Put children in pairs. They ask one another the two questions and then draw a picture of their partner wearing their favorite colors. Finally, children present their drawings and say: *His / Her name is ... His / Her favorite color is ...*

Unit 3 41

 **Look. Draw. Say.**

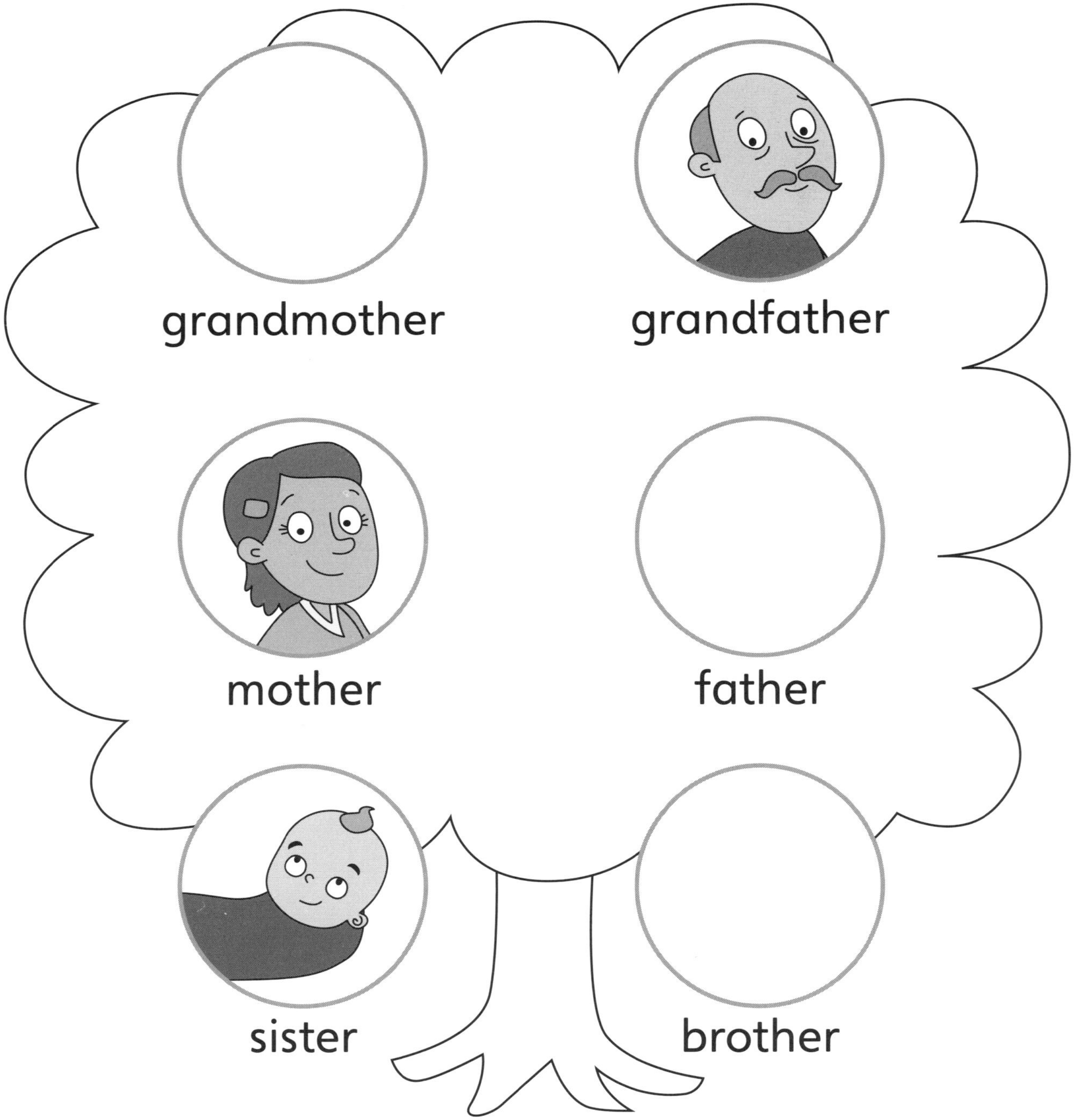

Cross-curricular: Social Studies

grandmother — grandfather

mother — father

sister — brother

Social Studies: Identifying family members. Look at the picture of the family on the left and ask: *Who's this?* Invite children to point to particular people and say: *He's the (brother).* Then focus on the family tree. Point to the blank circle at the top and read the label under it. Children repeat after you. Say: *This is the … (Grandmother.)* Children draw the grandmother from the family in the circle. Repeat with the other people. Finally, children point to the people in the family tree and say who they are.

Unit 3

 Count. Match. Trace.

Numeracy

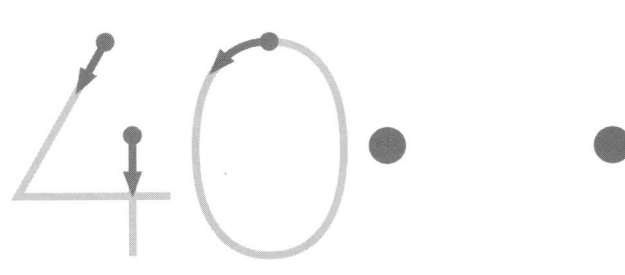

Numeracy: *forty*. Point to the first group of people and ask: *How many people can you see?* Count the people in the first row (10), then say: *Let's count by tens*. Children count and answer, then match the group to the correct number and trace the number. Continue with the other group. Finally, children practice counting by tens to forty.

Unit 3 — 43

 Say. Circle. Draw. Color. Review

How are we the same and different?

My favorite word in Unit 3 is:

Unit 3

Vocabulary and Language Review: Ask the Big Question: *How are we the same and different?* Children look back through Unit 3 to recall what they have learned. Ask children to look at the 10 pictures from Unit 3. They say the words then circle the pictures that they are able to name. Accept all possible answers. Then ask: *What is your favorite word in this unit?* Remind children of the words from the vocabulary lessons. Children draw a picture of their favorite word. They then present their pictures to the class saying: *My favorite word is … .* Answer the Big Question together, using their drawings and the pictures on the left as prompts. Finally, focus on the self-assessment activity. Ask: *How did you do in this unit?* Children color the face that shows how they feel they did.

4 What is a wild animal?

 Stick.   Match.   Say.   Trace.

bear   tiger   elephant   monkey   giraffe   lion

Vocabulary: *monkey, lion, giraffe, tiger, bear, elephant.* Point to each picture and say the word. Children point to the pictures and repeat after you. Say: *(Tiger / Monkey). Stick the (tiger / monkey).* Children stick each sticker as you say it. Then point to the first word on the left and say: *Bear.* Children repeat and draw a line to match the word with the correct picture. Repeat with the other words. They then point to each word and say the animal. Finally, children trace the words. Children can color the animals in colors of their preference.

Unit 4 45

😮 Say. ✓ Mark.

Story

Language: *Is there (a rhino) in the story? Yes, there is. / No, there isn't.* **rhino, tiger, elephant, lion, bear, monkey.** Point to the first picture. Ask: *Is there a rhino in the story? (Yes, there is.)* Elicit what children remember about this animal in the story. They put a check mark in the box next to the picture. Repeat with the other animals. Children put a check mark next to the animals that are in the story (the rhino, the tiger, the elephant, and the bear).

 Say.  Match.  Trace.

Phonics

S<u>ue</u>

●

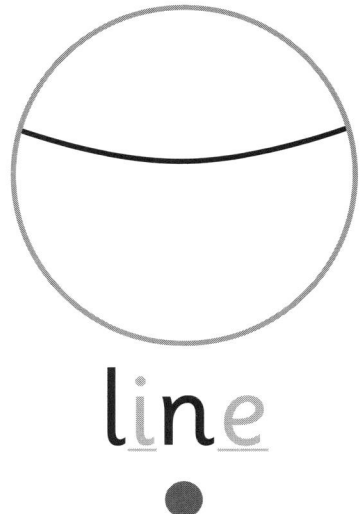

l<u>i</u>n<u>e</u>

●

c<u>a</u>k<u>e</u>

●

●

w<u>ai</u>t

●

r<u>u</u>l<u>e</u>

●

t<u>i</u>e

Phonics: *Sue, rule* /uː/. Point to each picture and say the word. Children repeat. Point to the picture of Sue and say the word, emphasizing the /uː/ sound. Say: *What sounds like Sue?* (*Rule.*) Repeat with the other words. Children draw lines to match the pairs of rhyming words. Finally, children trace the letters that make the sounds, saying the words as they do so.

Unit 4 47

 Look. Match. Say. Color. **Literacy**

First Next Last

Do you like the story?

Literacy: Identifying the sequence of a story. Ask children to think about the story and remember what happens. Look at the words at the top of the page and read them aloud. Children repeat. Point to the first scene and ask: *Is this picture first in the story? (No.)* Ask: *Which picture is first?* Children point to the correct scene. They draw a line to match the word to the scene. Repeat with *next* and *last*. Children then retell the story, using the scenes for reference. Finally, ask: *Do you like the story?* Children color the face that shows their opinion of the story.

 **Look.**  **Say.**  **Match.**

Values

Values: Learning to take care of wild animals. Point to the first picture and ask: *Are they taking care of wild animals? (Yes.) What are they doing?* Elicit ideas. Ask: *What animal are they taking care of?* Children point to the correct animal (the turtle). Repeat with the other pictures. Children draw lines to match the pictures.

Unit 4 49

 Point. Say.  Follow.  Trace.

Vocabulary

eagle   kangaroo   toucan   snake   shark   whale

 Unit 4

Vocabulary: *snake, whale, eagle, shark, kangaroo, toucan.* Children point to each animal's head, name the animal, and then follow the path to the body of the animal with their finger. Then, they use a crayon to draw the path, using a different color for each animal. Finally, children trace the words.

 Look. Draw. Say.

Language

Language: *Where does (a snake) go? On land. In the (air).* Look at the scene together and have children point to and name the different places *(land, water, air)*. Children look at each animal and draw it in the correct place in the scene (in the air, on land, or in the water). Then, they say where each animal goes: *The (toucan) goes (in the air)*.

Unit 4 51

 Count. Draw. Write. Say.

Concept

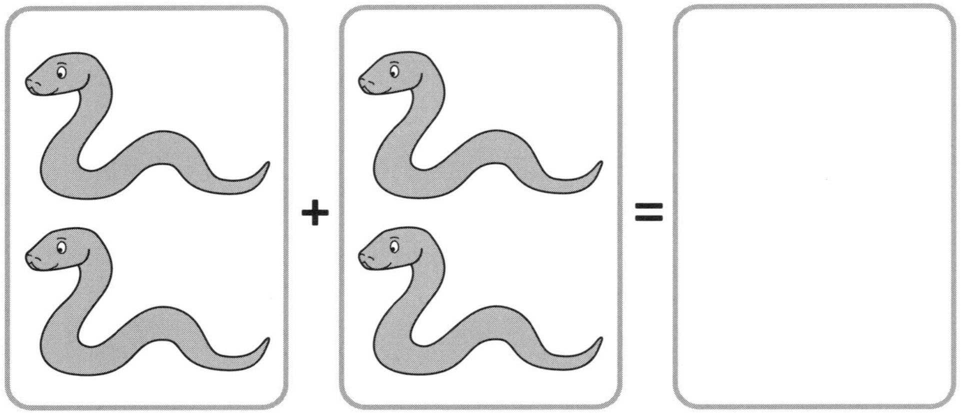

2 + 2 = 4

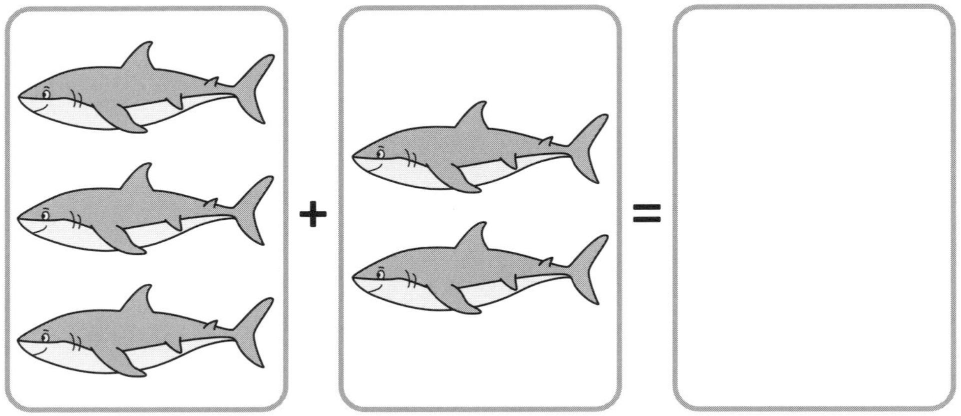

3 + 2 =

1 + 3 =

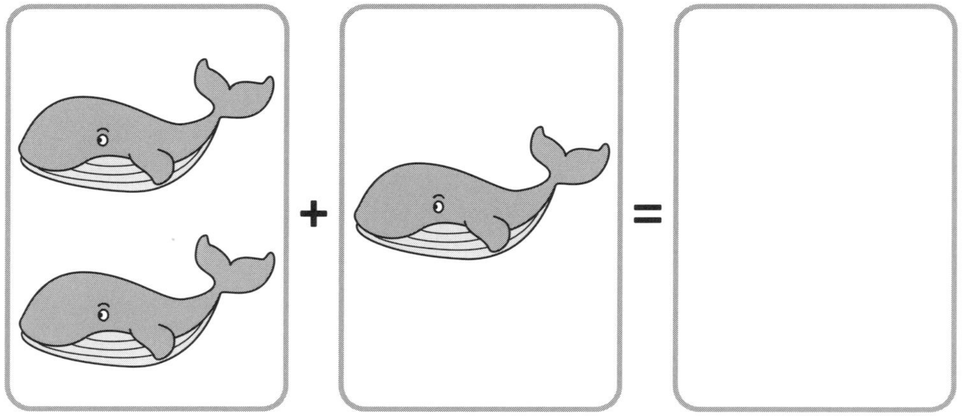

2 + 1 =

Concept: Adding together two sets of animals. Look at the first math problem with children. Ask: *How many snakes are there?* Point to the frames and encourage the children to count the snakes. Then point to the numbers and say: *Two plus two equals ...* Encourage children to answer. Once they agree on the number, children draw the total number in the box (four snakes). Finally, they say: *Two plus two equals four.* Continue with the other math problems. Children draw and write the total number for each math problem in the boxes.

52 Unit 4

 Look. Say.  Trace.

Vocabulary

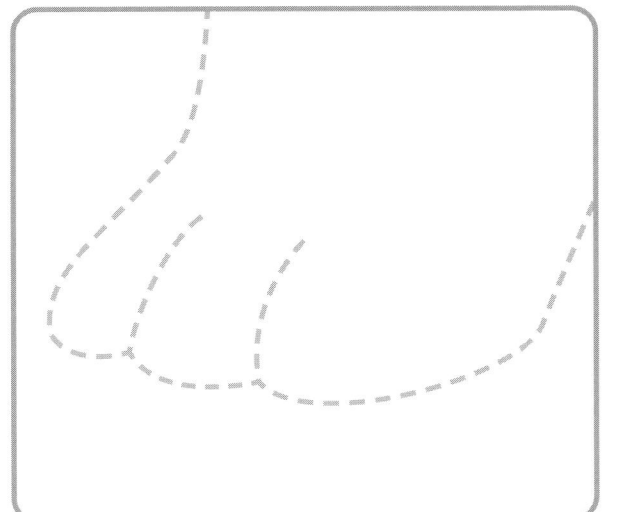

paw

fin

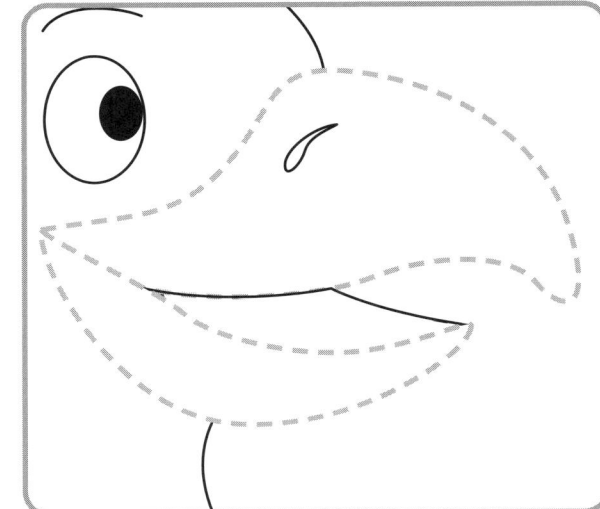

beak

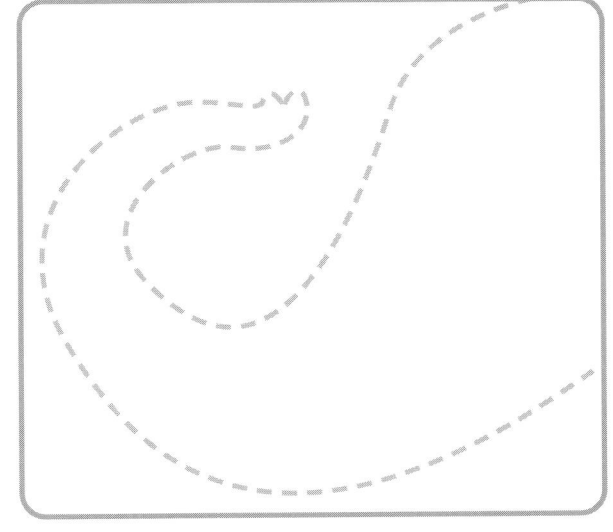

trunk

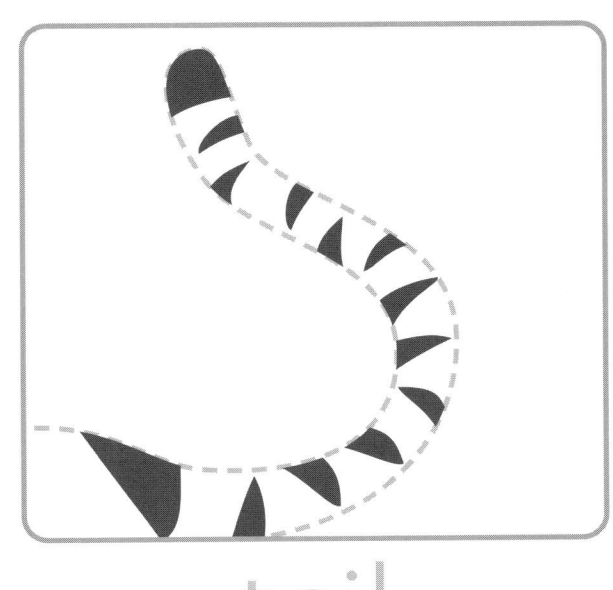

tail

wing

Vocabulary: *paw, fin, beak, trunk, tail, wing*. Children look at each picture and name the animal part. Then, they trace the animal part while repeating the word. Finally, children trace the words.

 Look. Say. Draw. Color.   Language

paw · fin · beak

trunk · tail · wing

Language: *What does (a shark) look like? It's (big) and (gray). It has a (long neck). It has (big paws).* Children look at each animal and name the missing part. Then, they draw the missing part and color in the animal. Finally, point to each animal and ask: *What does (a tiger) look like? (It's big. It's orange and black. It has a long tail. It has big paws.)*

✓ Mark. 💬 Talk.

Speaking

"Do you like monkeys?"

"Yes, I do."

"No, I don't."

Language: *Do you like (bears)? Yes, I do. No, I don't. Why? Why not? Because they're (cute / funny / scary). Because they have many colors.* Point to the monkeys and ask: *Do you like monkeys?* Repeat with the other animals. Children put a check mark in the boxes next to the animals they like. Focus on the speech bubbles and read the question and answers. Children repeat after you. Invite a confident child to the front and ask them: *Do you like (toucans)? Why (not)? Because they (have many colors).* Prompt them to use *because* if possible. Repeat with other volunteers. Children can then practice asking and answering the questions in pairs.

Unit 4   55

 Draw. Color. Say.

Cross-curricular: Science

This is a

It is ( ) and ( ).

It eats

It lives in the

 Count. Match. Trace.

Numeracy

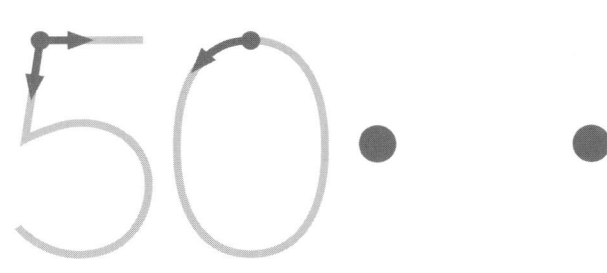

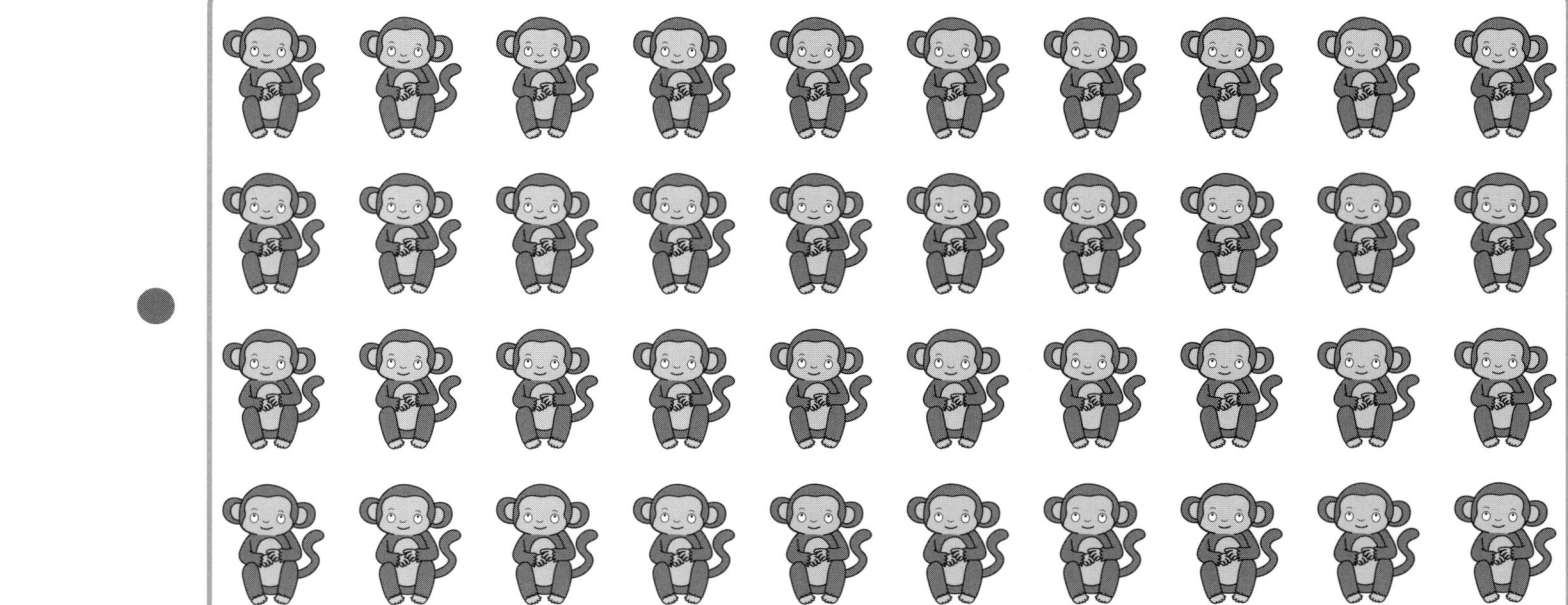

Numeracy: *fifty*. Point to the group of monkeys and ask: *How many monkeys can you see?* Count the monkeys in the first row (10), then say: *Let's count by tens.* Children count and answer, then match the group to the correct number, and trace the number. Repeat with the whales. Finally, children practice counting by tens to 50.

Unit 4 — 57

Say. Circle. Draw. Color. Review

What is a wild animal?

My favorite word in Unit 4 is:

Unit 4

Vocabulary and Language Review: Ask the Big Question: *What is a wild animal?* Children look back through Unit 4 to recall what they have learned. Ask children to look at the 10 pictures from Unit 4. They say the words then circle the pictures that they are able to name. Then ask: *What is your favorite word in this unit?* Remind children of the words from the vocabulary lessons. Children draw a picture of their favorite word. They then present their pictures to the class saying: *My favorite word is ... .* Answer the Big Question together, using their drawings and the pictures on the left as prompts. Finally, focus on the self-assessment activity. Ask: *How did you do in this unit?* Children color the face that shows how they feel they did.

5 Who helps our community?

● Stick. ✏ Write. ◡ Say. ✏ Trace.

1 2 3 4 5 6

cashier   chef   firefighter   mail carrier   police officer   doctor

Vocabulary: *firefighter, doctor, chef, police officer, mail carrier, cashier.* Point to each picture and say the word. Children point to the pictures and repeat after you. Say: *(Police officer / Cashier). Stick the (police officer / cashier).* Children stick each sticker as you say it. Then point to the first word and say: *Cashier.* Children repeat. Then ask: *What number is the cashier? (Six.)* Children write number 6 in the box above the word *cashier.* Repeat with the other words. They point to each word and say the job. Finally, children trace the words. Children can color the scene in colors of their preference.

Unit 5 59

◯ Circle. ◡ Say.   Story

1 2 3 4

1 2 3 4

1 2 3 4

1 2 3 4

Language: *Is this picture (first) in the story? Which picture is (first)?* Look at the scenes from the story. Point to the first scene and ask: *Is this picture first in the story? (No.)* Ask: *Which picture is first?* Children point to the correct scene. They circle the number 1 under the scene to show that it is the first. Repeat with the second, third, and last scenes. Children then retell the story, using the scenes for reference.

 Say. ✓ Mark. ✏ Trace.

Phonics

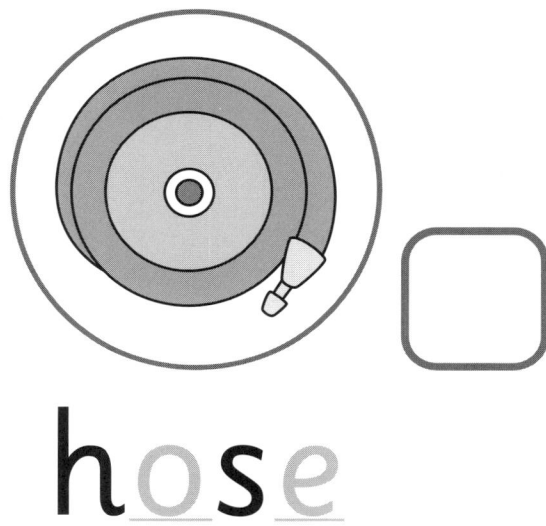
hose

snow

rule

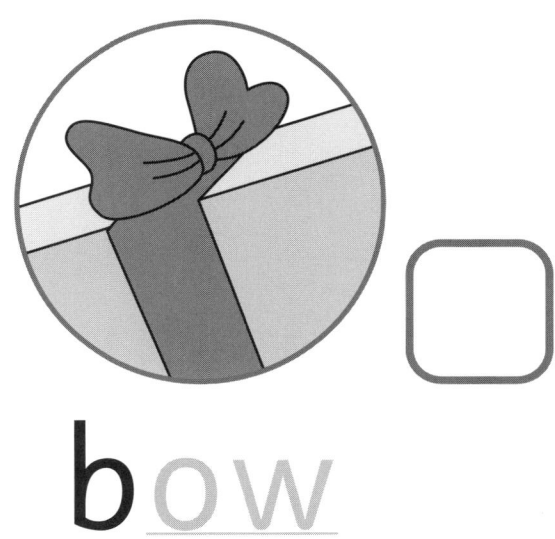
bow

tie

nose

Phonics: *snow, bow, hose* /oʊ/. Point to each picture and say the word. Children repeat. Point to *hose* and say the word, emphasizing the /oʊ/ sound. Then point to *snow*. Say: /oʊ/, *snow*. Same sound? (Yes.) Repeat with *rule* (No.) Children put a check mark in the boxes next to the pictures with the /oʊ/ sound. Finally, children trace the letters that make the /oʊ/ sound, saying the words as they do so.

Unit 5 61

 Look. Color.

Literacy

 =   =  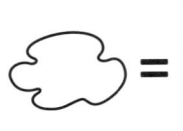 =

 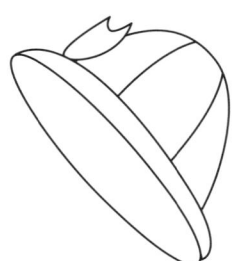  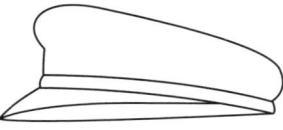

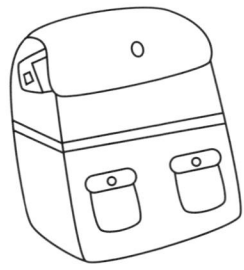 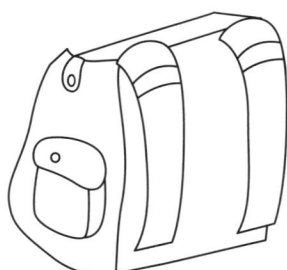 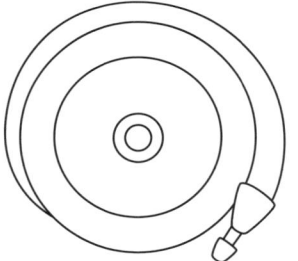

Do you like the story?

Unit 5

Literacy: Identifying details from a story. Ask children to think about the story and remember what happens. Children choose four colors to represent the four characters and complete the key at the top of the page. They then look at the pictures of the items from the story, decide who each one belongs to, and color each picture according to their key. Finally, ask: *Do you like the story?* Children color the face that shows their opinion of the story.

 Values

Values: Saying thank you to people who help you. Point to the people at the table. Ask: *Who is saying thank you? Is the waiter saying thank you? (No.) Is the boy saying thank you? (Yes.)* Discuss when we say thank you, and who to. Finally, children identify and color the people who are saying thank you.

Unit 5 63

 Say. Trace. Write.

Vocabulary

| hospital | restaurant | post office | fire station |

grocery store

r_____

p___ _____

police station

h_____

f___ _____

 **Point.**  **Follow.** **Say.**

Language

Language: *Where does a (chef) work? A (chef) works in a (restaurant).* Children point to the first worker and name the job. Ask: *Where does a doctor work?* Children follow the path through the maze to find the workplace, point to it, and answer: *A hospital.* They then draw a line to match the doctor to the hospital. Repeat with the other workers. Finally, children ask and answer in pairs about where each person works: *Where does a (doctor) work? A (doctor) works in a (hospital).*

 Count. Say. Draw. Trace.

Concept

- ⚃ + ☐ = 10
- ☐ + ⚀ = 6
- ⚅ + ☐ = 8
- ⚃ + ☐ = 7
- ☐ + ⚀ = 2
- ☐ + ⚁ = 5

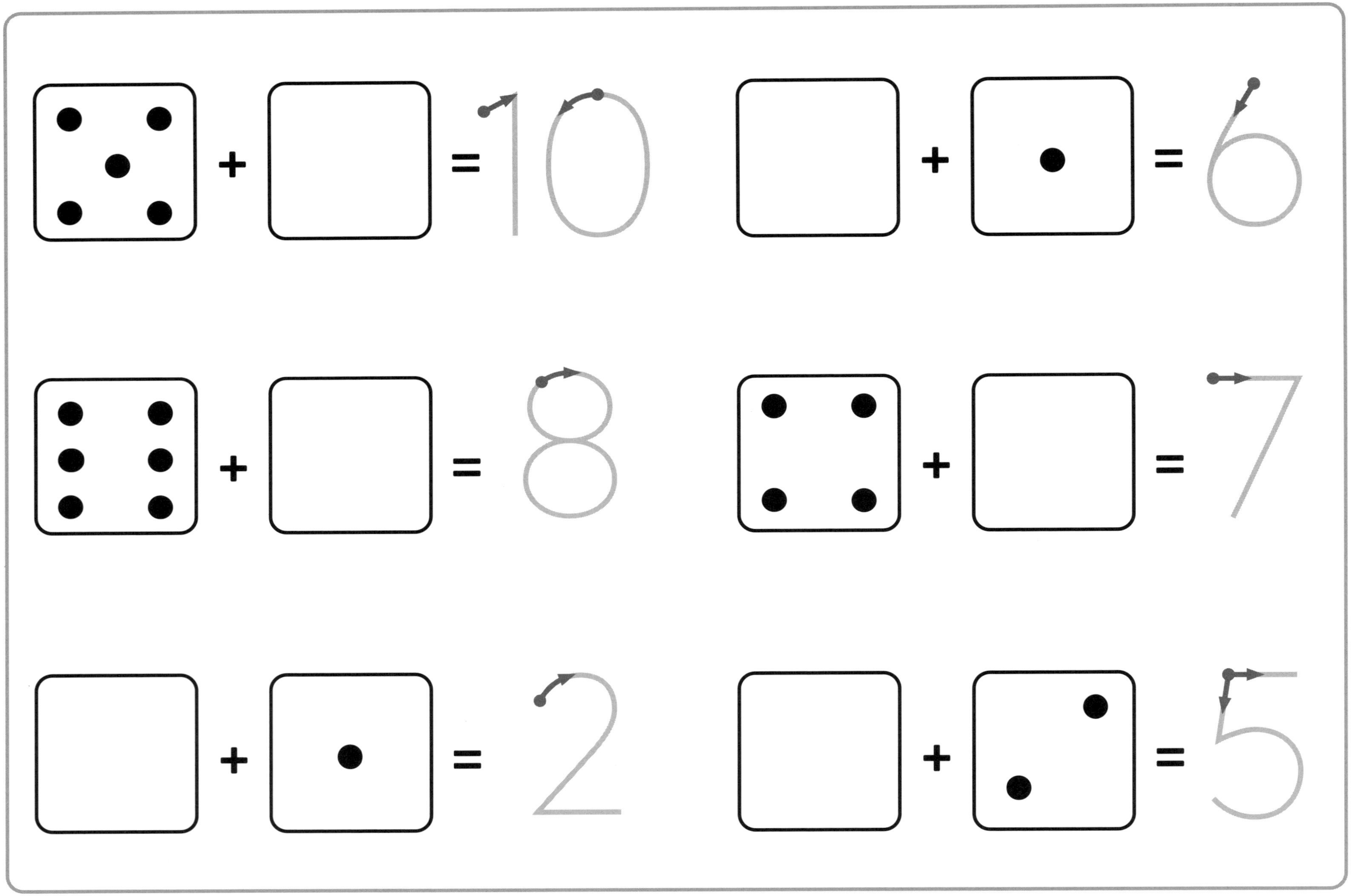

Concept: Adding two quantities together to make a total. Look at the first pair of dice, and the total after it. Say: *Ten*. Point to the first dice and ask children to count the dots on it. Then ask: *How many more do we need to make ten?* (*Five.*) Children draw the missing dots on the dice and trace the number. Repeat with the other math problems.

 Match.  Say.  Trace.

Vocabulary

cook food

take care of people

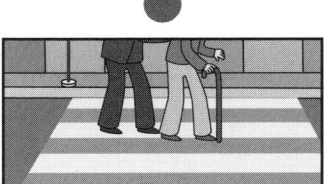
keep people safe

ring up groceries

put out fires

deliver mail

Vocabulary: *put out fires, take care of people, cook food, keep people safe, deliver mail, ring up groceries.* Children draw lines to match the tops and bottoms of each picture, then say the phrases. Finally, children trace the words.

Unit 5 67

 Count. Say. Color.

START

Language

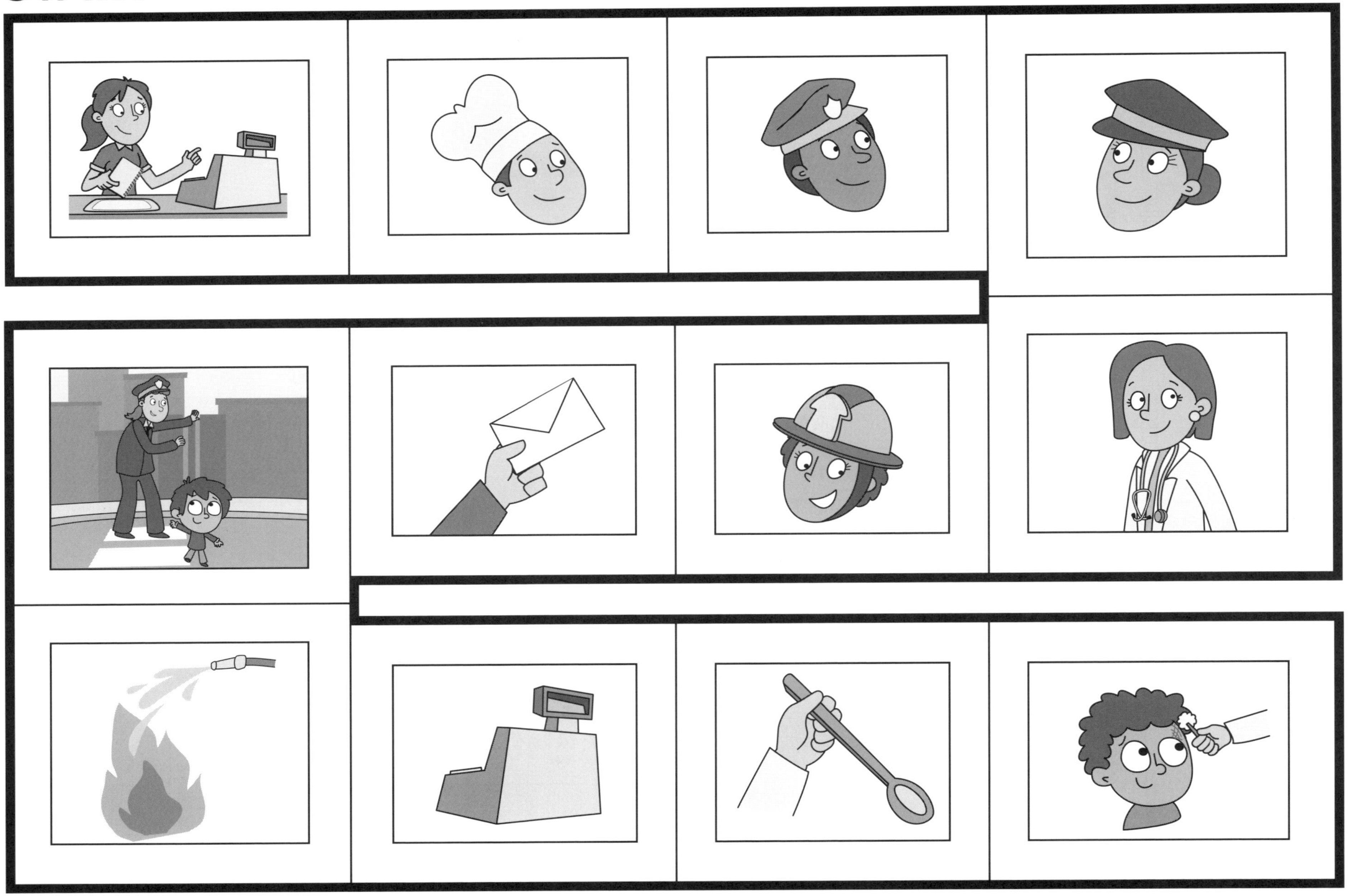

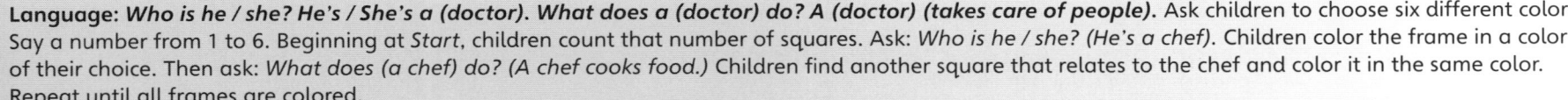

Language: *Who is he / she? He's / She's a (doctor). What does a (doctor) do? A (doctor) (takes care of people).* Ask children to choose six different colors. Say a number from 1 to 6. Beginning at *Start*, children count that number of squares. Ask: *Who is he / she? (He's a chef).* Children color the frame in a color of their choice. Then ask: *What does (a chef) do? (A chef cooks food.)* Children find another square that relates to the chef and color it in the same color. Repeat until all frames are colored.

68 Unit 5

 **Think. Draw. Say.**

Speaking

What do you want to be?

I want to be a chef.

Language: *What do you want to be? I want to be a (chef). Why? I love (food)!* Point to the pictures and have children name the jobs. Then point to and read the speech bubbles. Children repeat. Ask: *What do you want to be?* Elicit their ideas, and help with language as necessary. Encourage them to tell you why they want to do each job. Children draw themselves doing their chosen job. Invite children to the front to present their work and explain what they want to be and why.

Unit 5

 **Look. Say. Cross.**

Cross-curricular: Social Studies

firefighter

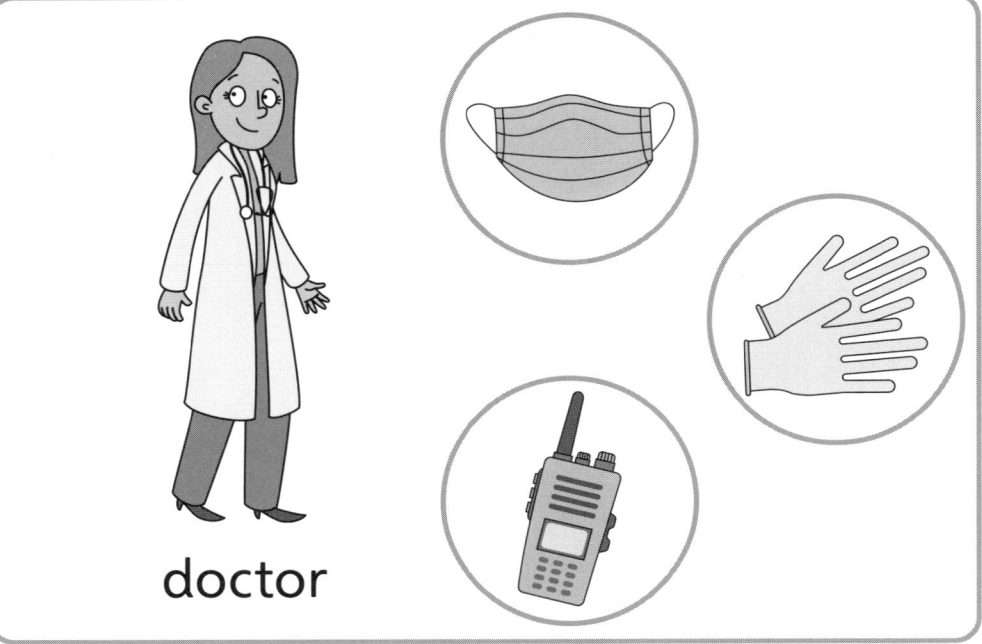

doctor

chef

police officer

Social Studies: Learning about safety at work. Point to the picture of the firefighter and read the word. Children repeat. Point to the helmet and ask: *Does the firefighter need this? (Yes.) Why?* Discuss with children how the item helps to protect the person. Repeat with the jacket *(Yes)* and the glove *(No)*. Children cross out the glove. Repeat with the other people and items.

¹²₃ Count. Color. Trace.

Numeracy

10   20   30   40   50   60

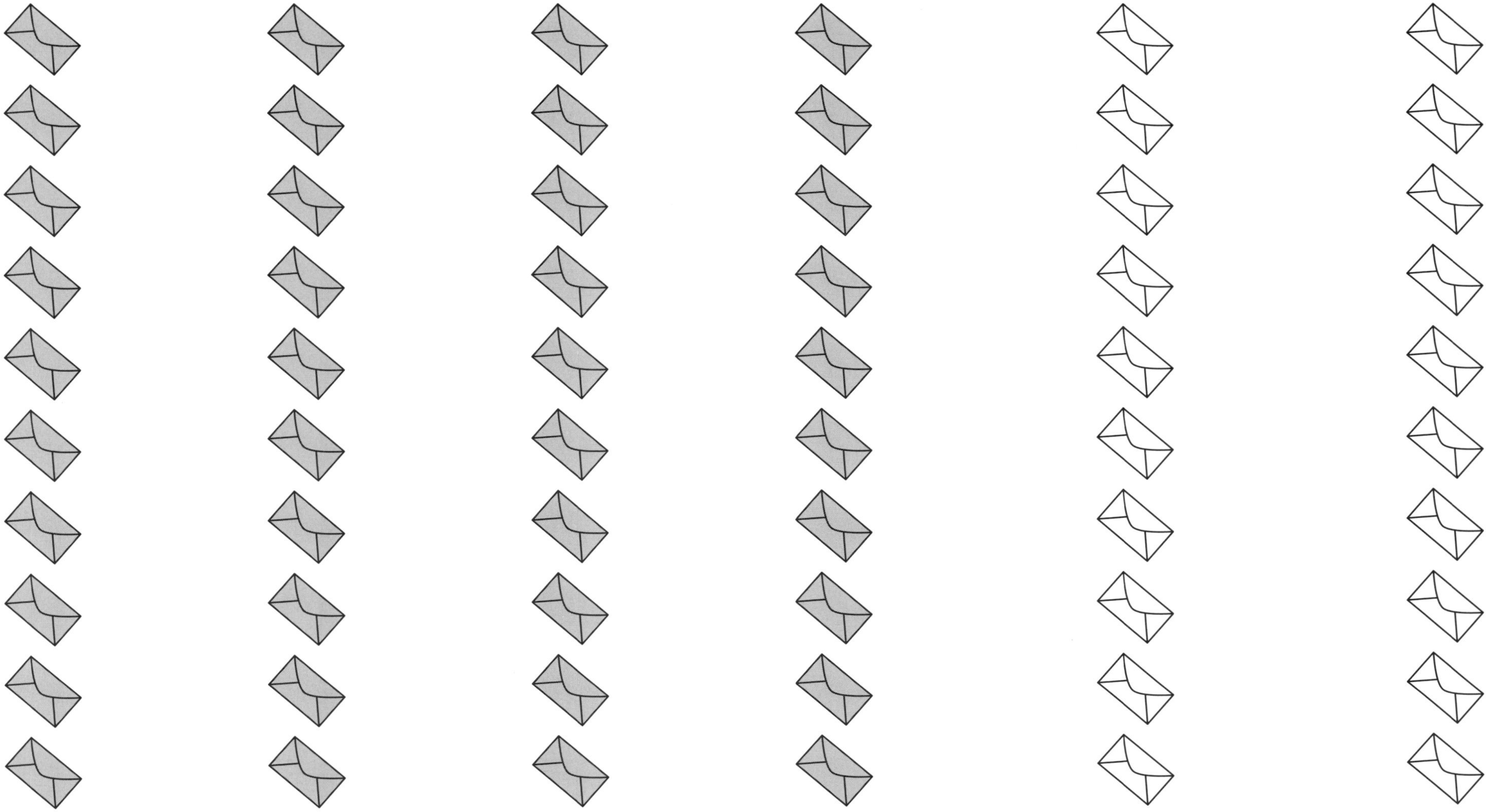

Numeracy: sixty. Point to the first column of letters and ask: *How many letters can you see?* Count the letters in the first column (10), then say: *Let's count by tens.* Children count and answer, then color the letters in the last two columns and trace numbers 50 and 60. Finally, children practice counting by tens to sixty.

Unit 5

Say. Circle. Draw. Color.

Review

Who helps our community?

My favorite word in Unit 5 is:

Unit 5

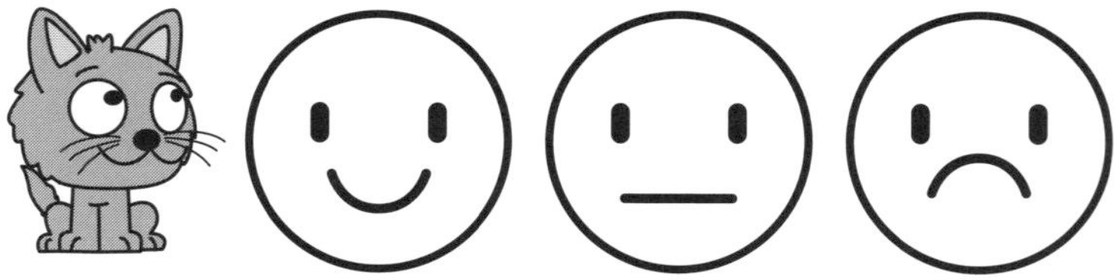

Vocabulary and Language Review: Ask the Big Question: *Who helps our community?* Children look back through Unit 5 to recall what they have learned. Ask children to look at the 10 pictures from Unit 5. They say the words then circle the pictures that they are able to name. Accept all possible answers. Then ask: *What is your favorite word in this unit?* Remind children of the words from the vocabulary lessons. Children write and draw a picture of their favorite word. If necessary, write the words on the board for children to copy. Children present their pictures to the class saying: *My favorite word is ... .* Answer the Big Question together, using their drawings and the pictures on the left as prompts. Finally, focus on the self-assessment activity. Ask: *How did you do in this unit?* Children color the face that shows how they feel they did.

6. What do we do in restaurants?

 Stick. Say.  Match. Trace.

menu

drink

waiter

dessert

main dish

side dish

◯ Circle. ◡ Say.

Story

1 2 3 4

1 2 3 4

1 2 3 4

1 2 3 4

Language: *Is this picture (first) in the story? Which picture is (first)?* Look at the scenes from the story. Point to the first scene and ask: *Is this picture first in the story?* (No.) Ask: *Which picture is first?* Children point to the correct scene. They circle the number 1 under the scene to show that it is the first. Repeat with the second, third, and last scenes. Children then retell the story, using the scenes for reference.

Say. Follow. Trace.  Phonics

eat	meet	tie	hose
cake	bee	read	train
rule	Sue	teach	tree

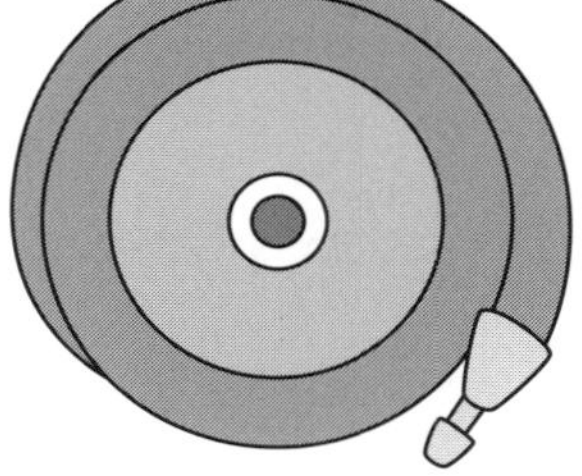

Phonics: *meet, eat, teach, see* /iː/. Point to each picture and say the word. Children repeat. Point to *eat*, and say the word, emphasizing the /iː/ sound. Say: /iː/, *eat*. Same sound? (Yes.) Repeat with *meet* (Yes) and *tie* (No). Children draw the path through the maze, moving only to words with the /iː/ sound. Finally, children trace the letters that make the /iː/ sound, saying the words as they do so.

Unit 6

 Say. Match. Draw. Color.

Literacy

1 Where does the story take place?

2 What happens at the restaurant?

3 Who are the four characters?

Do you like the story?

👁 **Look.** 😃 **Say.** ✏ **Color.**

Values

Values: Being polite. Point to one of the children being polite. Ask: *Is he / she being polite?* Then point to a child not being polite and repeat. Discuss why not and what the child could do better. Finally, children identify and color the children who are being polite.

Unit 6

 Say. Trace.  Write. Color.

Vocabulary

1. soda
2. beans
3. steak
4. rice
5. lemonade
6. French fries

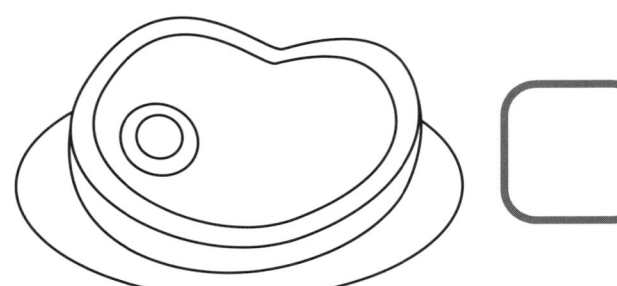
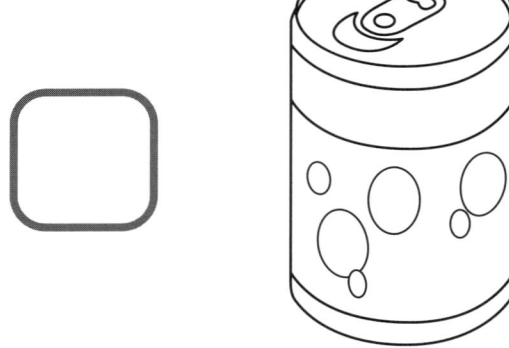

Vocabulary: *steak, beans, lemonade, rice, soda, French fries.* Point to each picture and have children name the food or drink, and mime eating or drinking it. Repeat several times. Point to the first word and say: *One. Soda.* Children repeat and trace the word. Say it again and have children find the corresponding picture and write the number 1 in the box. Repeat with the other words. Finally, children can color their favorite food and drink.

Unit 6

 **Look.** **Say.** **Color.** **Draw.**

Language

 She likes lemonade.

 She doesn't like lemonade.

 She likes French fries.

 She doesn't like French fries.

 He likes beans.

 He doesn't like beans.

 I like steak.

 I don't like steak.

Language: *(She) likes (beans). She / He doesn't like (lemonade). Do you like steak? Yes, I do. No, I don't. I like steak. I don't like steak.* Point to the first picture and read the two sentences, making a happy and a sad face each time. Children mime and repeat. Then ask: *Does she like lemonade? (No.)* Point to the sentence and sad face and say: *She doesn't like lemonade.* Children repeat and color the correct face. Repeat with the other pictures. For the last one, children decide which sentence is true for themselves. They draw themselves with a steak in the box and color the correct face.

Unit 6

 Count. Say. Draw.

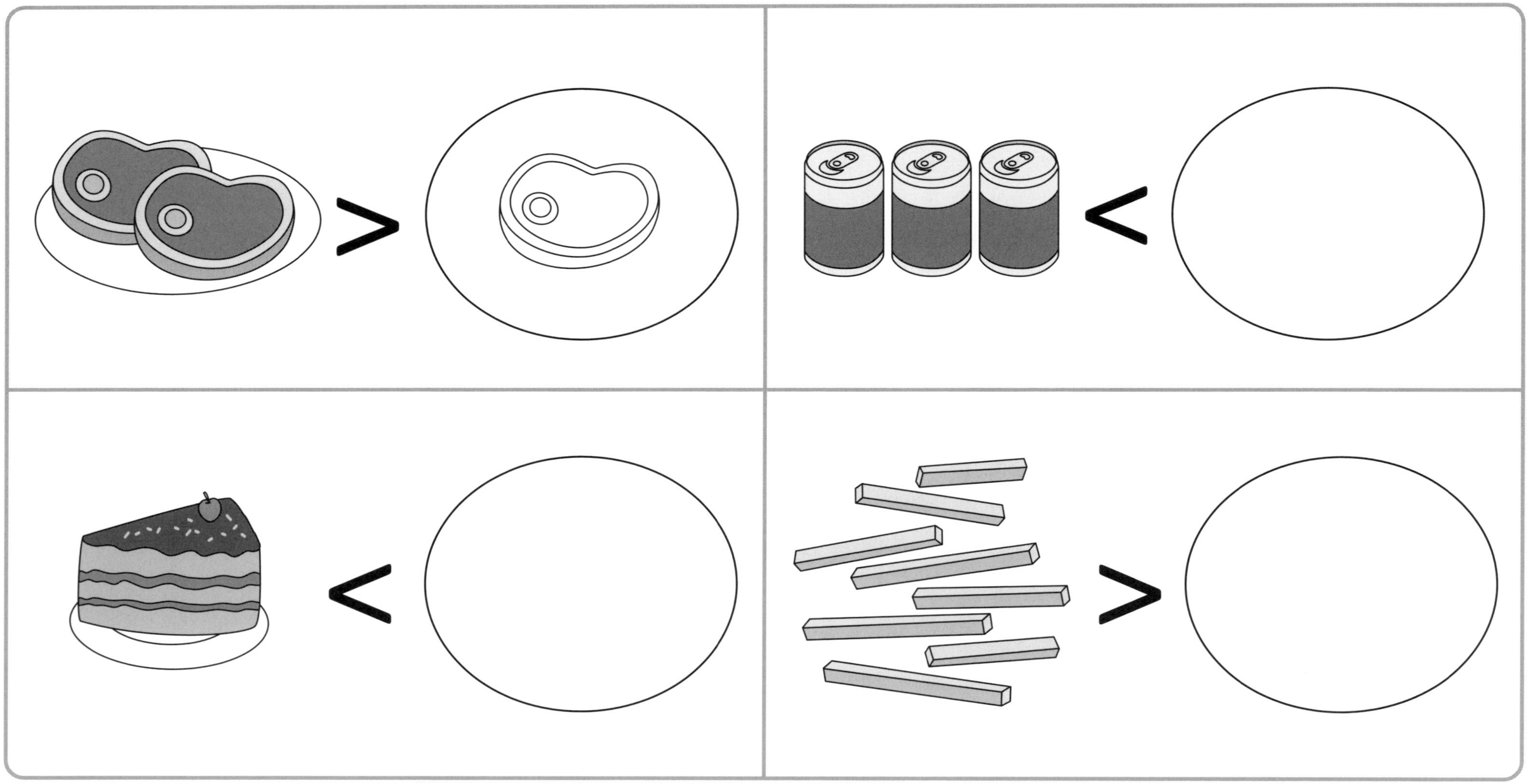

Concept

Concept: more, less. Review the signs <, >. Use the language *Less than* and *More than*. Direct children's attention to the first picture. Point and say: *How many? Let's count.* Count the steaks together as a class. Then point to the sign. Ask: *Do we need more than two, or less than two here?* (Less than.) *What is less than two?* (One.) Draw children's attention to the example steak on the plate. Children say: *One is less than two*. Repeat with the other plates. Children draw a correct number of the food or drink on each plate. Accept all possible answers.

 Say. Trace. Write. Color.

Vocabulary

cheeseburger   pizza   vegetables   ice cream

chocolate cake

p_____

i__ _____

spaghetti

v_____

c_____

Vocabulary: *spaghetti, pizza, ice cream, chocolate cake, vegetables, cheeseburger.* Point to the picture of the chocolate cake and say: *What's this?* Children answer and trace the word. Repeat with the picture of the spaghetti. Then point to and read the words in the box at the top. Children repeat after you, pointing to each word as they say it. Point to the picture of the pizza and say: *What's this?* Children answer and trace the first letter, then write the rest of the word. Repeat with the other pictures. Finally, they color the pictures of the food they like.

Unit 6 81

👁 Look. 👄 Say. ✏ Color.

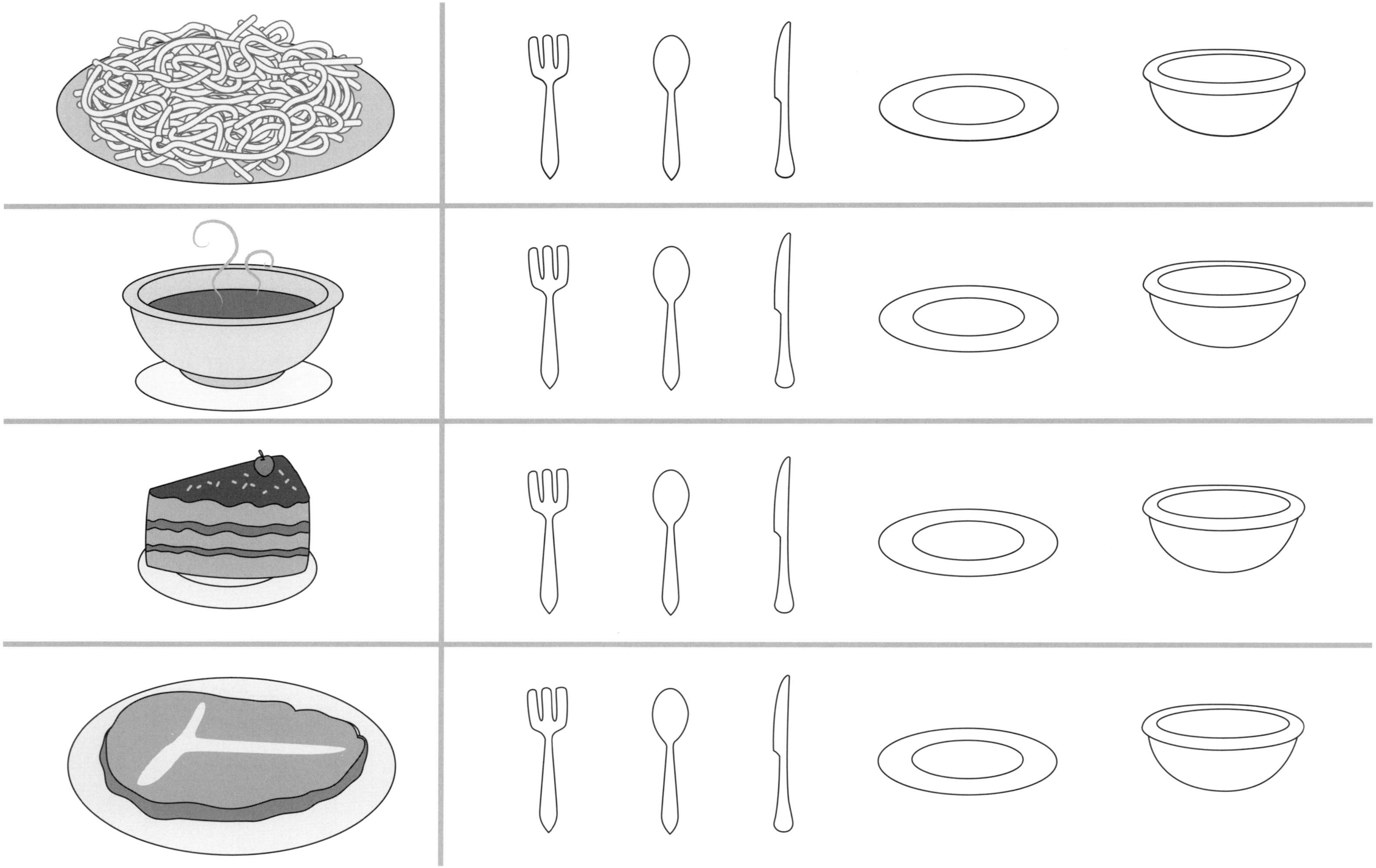

Language

Language: *What do we need to eat (spaghetti)? We need a (fork / spoon / knife) and a (plate / bowl) to eat (spaghetti).* Children look at each food item and name it. Ask: *What do we need to eat spaghetti?* Elicit answers using the language: *We need a fork and a plate to eat spaghetti.* Children color the fork and plate in the top row. Note there are different possible answers and allow children to share how they eat different foods. Continue in the same manner with the remaining food items.

82 Unit 6

 Draw. Say.

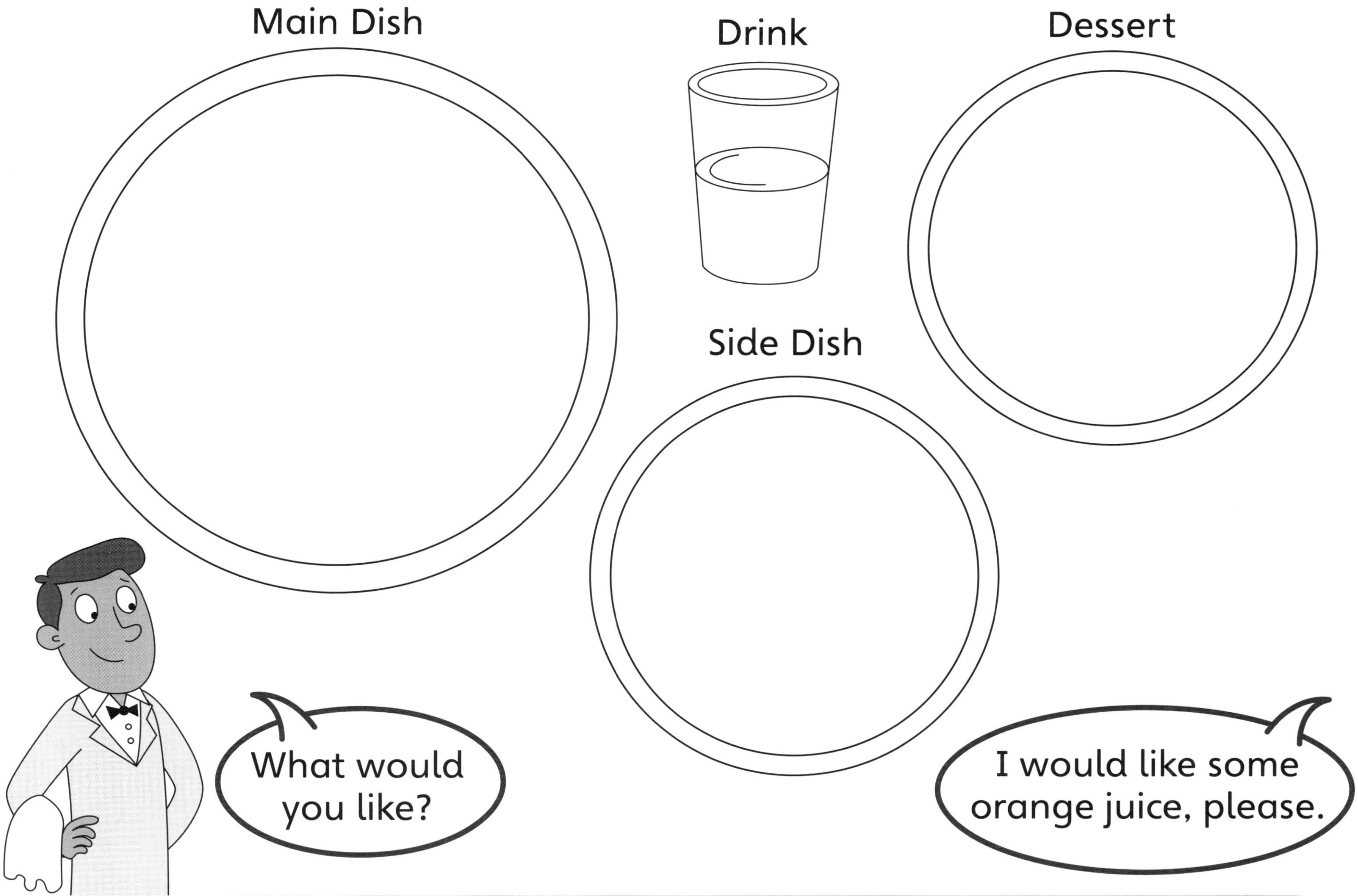

Speaking

Main Dish

Drink

Dessert

Side Dish

What would you like?

I would like some orange juice, please.

Language: *What would you like to (drink)? I would like some (orange juice), please. Would you like a (main dish)? Yes, please. Anything for dessert? Some (chocolate cake), please.* Read the speech bubbles and have children repeat after you. Then read the labels and elicit ideas for foods and drinks for each section. Children draw and color what they would like to eat and drink for each part of the meal. Ask individual children to share their pictures with the class and say what they would like to eat and drink, using the language: *I would like (pizza, orange juice, and ice cream), please.* Children can then practice acting out ordering in a restaurant in pairs or groups.

Unit 6 83

👁 Look. ✨ Match. ✏ Draw. ◠ Say.   Cross-curricular: Science

  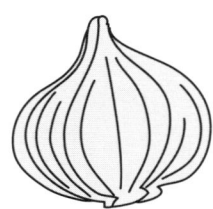   

banana   pineapple   onion   broccoli   grapes   lettuce

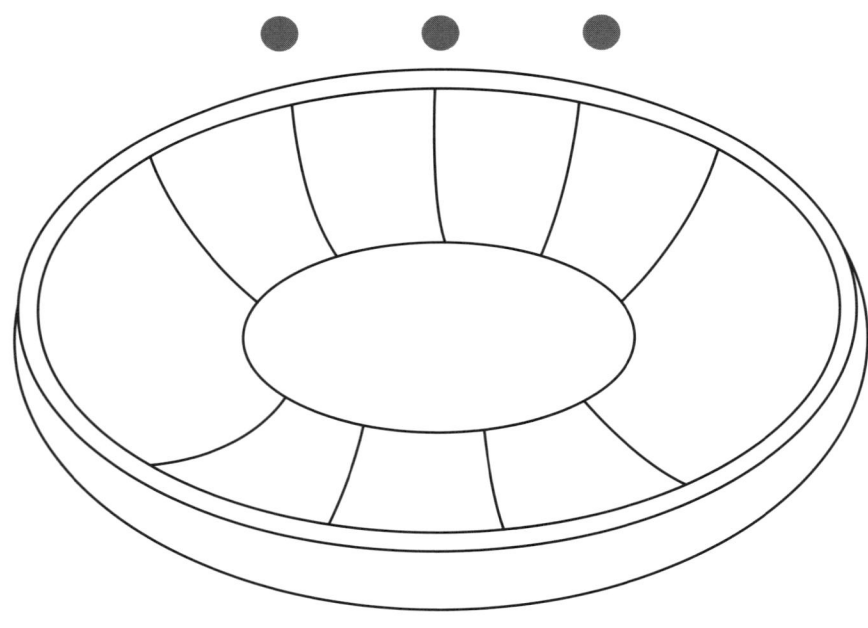

fruit

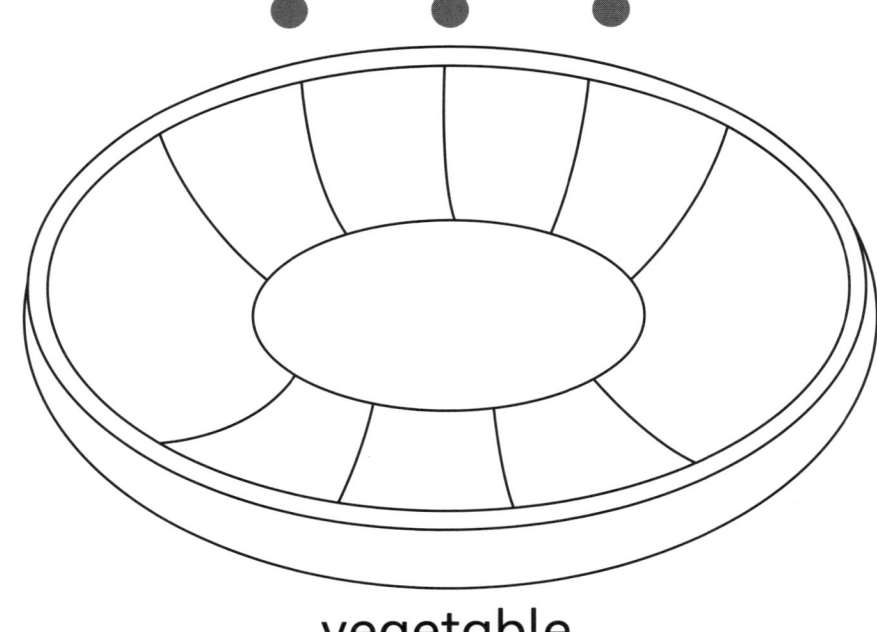

vegetable

Science: Categorizing food as a fruit or a vegetable. Point to the labels under the baskets. Read the first one *(fruit)* and then the second one *(vegetable)*. Then point to the banana and ask: *What is it? (A banana.) Is it a fruit or a vegetable? (A fruit.)* Children draw a line to match the banana to the fruit basket. Repeat with the other fruits and vegetables. Then ask children to think and draw two more fruits and vegetables in the correct basket. Finally, children point to and describe what they have drawn.

 Count. Color. Trace.

Numeracy

10 20 30 40 50 60 70

Numeracy: *seventy*. Point to the first column of bananas and ask: *How many bananas can you see?* Count the bananas in the first column (10), then say: *Let's count by tens.* Children count and answer, then color the bananas in the last two columns and trace numbers 60 and 70. Finally, children practice counting by tens to seventy.

Unit 6 85

Say. Circle. Draw. Color. Review

What do we do in restaurants?

My favorite word in Unit 6 is:

Unit 6

Vocabulary and Language Review: Ask the Big Question: *What do we do in restaurants?* Children look back through Unit 6 to recall what they have learned. Ask children to look at the 10 pictures from Unit 6. They say the words then circle the pictures that they are able to name. Accept all possible answers. Then ask: *What is your favorite word in this unit?* Remind children of the words from the vocabulary lessons. Children write and draw a picture of their favorite word. If necessary, write the words on the board for children to copy. Children present their pictures to the class saying: *My favorite word is … .* Answer the Big Question together, using their drawings and the pictures on the left as prompts. Finally, focus on the self-assessment activity. Ask: *How did you do in this unit?* Children color the face that shows how they feel they did.

7 What is a routine?

 Stick.   Write.   Say.   Trace.

do homework

go to school

get up

have breakfast

go home

get dressed

Vocabulary: *get up, get dressed, have breakfast, go to school, go home, do homework.* Point to the first picture and say the phrase. Children point to the picture and repeat the phrase. Repeat with the other phrases. Say: *(Have breakfast / Get dressed).* Stick *(have breakfast / get dressed).* Children stick each sticker as you say it. Then ask: *What do you do first?* Children number the activities in the order they usually do them. Say: *1.* Children take turns to say the activity they do first. Repeat with numbers 2–6 and the rest of the activities. Finally, children trace the words. Children can color the pictures in colors of their preference.

Unit 7 87

 Color. Say.

Story

Language: *Is (Hare) (happy)? happy, sad.* Look at the scenes from the story. Point to Hare in the first scene and ask: *Who's this? (Hare.) Is (Hare) happy? (Yes.)* Children color the correct emoji. Repeat with the other scenes. Children then retell the story, using the scenes for reference.

Say. Follow. Write. — Phonics

| cl | cr |

__ __ ock

__ __ othes

__ __ y

Phonics: *clock, clothes* /kl/; *cry* /kr/ (consonant blends). Point to the consonant blends in the box and read them aloud. Children repeat, pointing to each consonant blend as they say it. Point to each picture and say the word. Children repeat. Point to the picture of clothes. Children follow the path with their finger to find the word. They then draw a line to match the picture to the word. Say the word again, emphasizing the /kl/ sound. Say: /kl/, *clothes*. Children point to the correct letters in the box at the top. They write the letters to complete the word. Repeat with the other pictures and words.

Unit 7 89

 **Look.**  **Match.**  **Say.**  **Color.**

Literacy

First
Next
Last

Do you like the story?

Literacy: Identifying the sequence of a story. Ask children to think about the story and remember what happens. Look at the words at the top of the page and read them aloud. Children repeat. Point to the first scene and ask: *Is this picture first in the story? (No.)* Ask: *Which picture is first?* Children point to the correct scene. They draw a line to match the word to the scene. Repeat with *next* and *last*. Children then retell the story, using the scenes for reference. Finally, ask: *Do you like the story?* Children color the face that shows their opinion of the story.

Unit 7

👁 Look. ✓ Mark. 😊 Say.

Values

Values: Having a routine. Point to the first picture and elicit the activity (do homework). Ask: *Is this in your routine? Do you do it every day?* If they do the activity every day, children put a check mark in the box. Then repeat with the second picture (have a party). Ask: *Do you do this every day?* Repeat with all the pictures. Children put a check mark in the boxes next to the activities they do every day. They point and say: *I (get up) every day.* Discuss with children the difference between activities in our routine and those we do sometimes.

Unit 7 91

Say. Trace. Write. Color.

Vocabulary

play   music

1 dance class

2 soccer practice

3 m____ lessons

4 swimming lessons

5 p___ with friends

6 gymnastics

Vocabulary: *dance class, soccer practice, music lessons, swimming lessons, play with friends, gymnastics.* Point to each picture and have children name and mime the activity. Repeat several times. Point to the first word and say: *One. Dance class.* Children repeat and trace the words. Say it again and have children find the corresponding picture and write the number 1 in the box. Repeat with the other words and phrases. For 3 and 5, they also write the missing words, using the words in the box to help them. Finally, children can color three activities they do.

Circle. Draw. Say. Write.

Language

He has music lessons.

She plays with friends.

He has soccer practice.

I _____.

Language: *What does he / she do after school? He / She (has dance class). He / She (plays with friends). What do you do after school? I (have swimming lessons).* Point to the first sentence and read it aloud. Children point and repeat after you. Elicit which picture is correct, and have children point, then circle the correct picture. Repeat with the other sentences. Then focus on the final section. Say: *And you? What do you do after school?* Elicit ideas. Children draw themselves doing an after-school activity, then complete the sentence. They can look at the Student's Book page to help with spelling.

Unit 7

 Count.  Cross.  Match. Write.

Concept

6 − 1 = ____

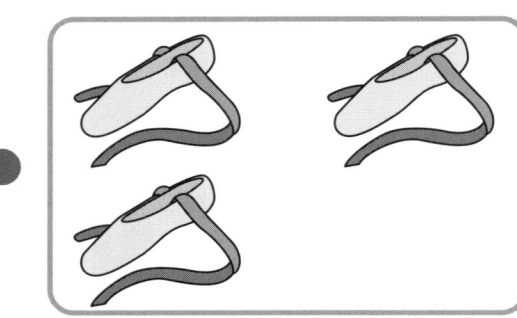

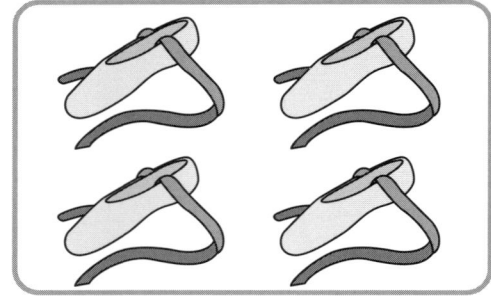

4 − 1 = ____

3 − 1 = ____

8 − 1 = ____

Concept: *Taking away one.* Point to the first picture and have children count the soccer balls. Then point to and read the first math problem aloud: *Six minus one equals ...* . Guide children to cross out the last soccer ball and count the remaining balls. They then draw a line to the correct picture on the right. Repeat the math problem including the answer: *Six minus one equals five.* Children repeat and write the answer. Repeat with the other math problems.

94 Unit 7

 Say. Trace. Write. Point.

Vocabulary

| take a bath | read a book | go to bed | eat dinner |

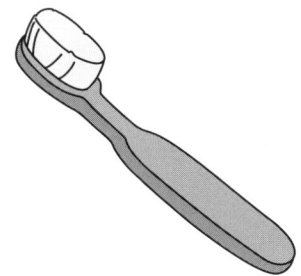

brush my teeth

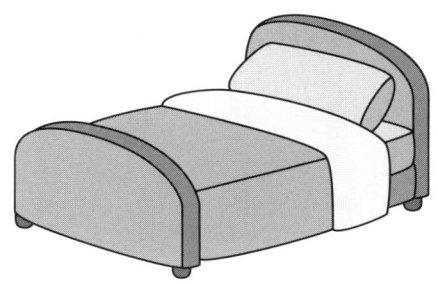

g_ __ ___

r___ _ ___

put on pajamas

e__ _____

t___ _ ___

Vocabulary: *eat dinner, take a bath, brush my teeth, put on pajamas, read a book, go to bed.* Point to the picture of the toothbrush and have children name the activity and trace the phrase. Repeat with the picture of the pajamas. Then point to and read the phrases in the box at the top. Children repeat after you, pointing to each phrase as they say it. Point to the picture of the bed and elicit the activity. Children trace the first letter, then write the rest of the phrase. Repeat with the other pictures. Children work in pairs, taking turns to point to an activity for their partner to name.

Unit 7 95

👁 **Look.** ✏️ **Write.** 😃 **Say.**

> Language

always   sometimes   never

1 I _____  in the evening.

2 I _____ 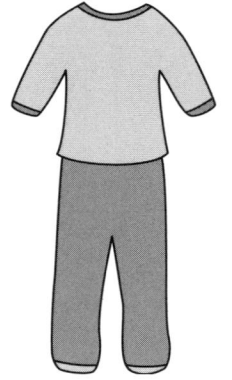 in the evening.

3 I _____ 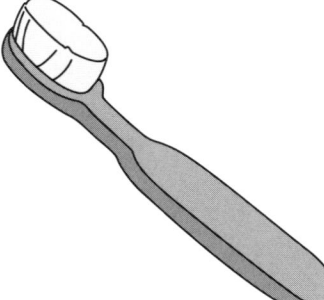 in the evening.

Language: *What do you do in the evening? I always / sometimes / never (put on pajamas).* Look at the word box together and read each word. Then ask children: *What do you do in the evening?* Have children follow along as you read each sentence to them: *I always, sometimes, or never (read a book) in the evening.* Children write the correct word according to their own routines. Finally, invite children to read their sentences for the class.

 Say. Circle. Talk.

Speaking

What do you want to do?

Let's paint!

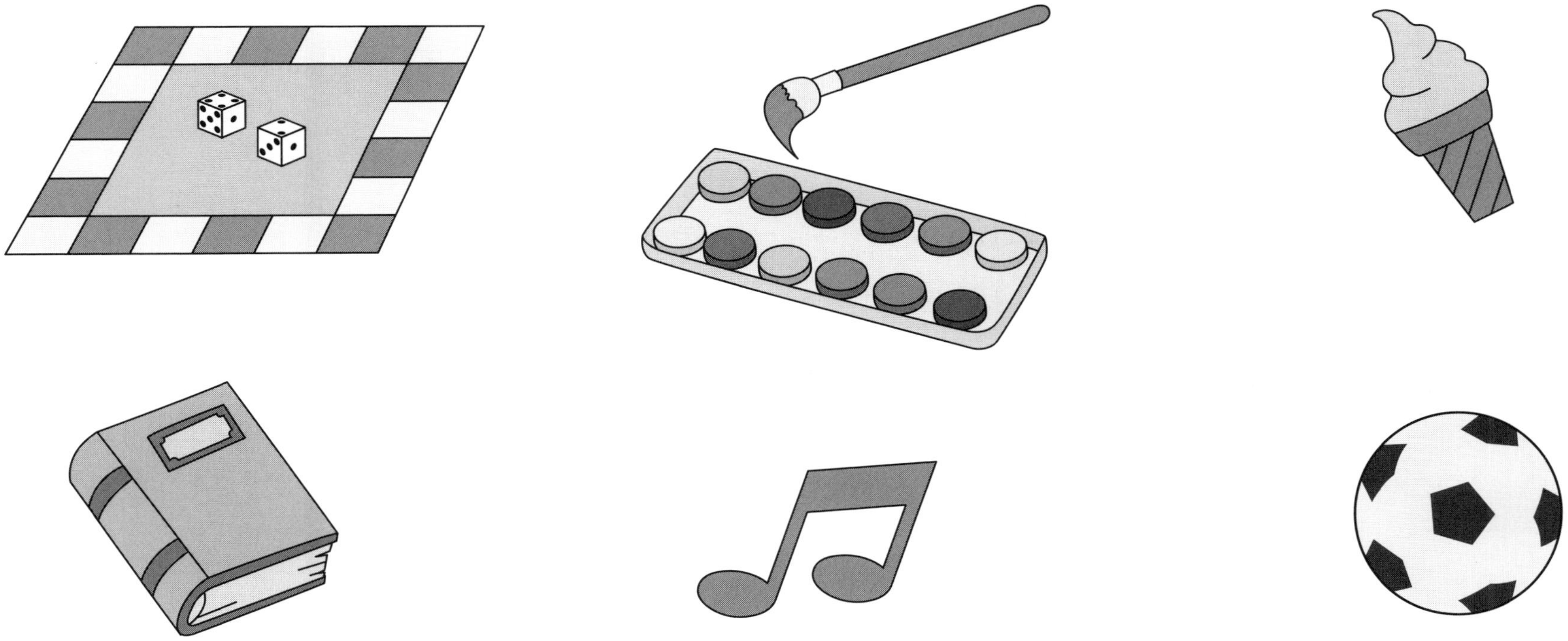

Language: *I'm bored. What do you want to do? I don't know. Let's (paint).* Point to Leo and Mia and read the question and answer aloud. Children repeat. Look at the pictures in the box and elicit the activities. Children choose one activity they want to do and circle it. Children move around the classroom asking and answering the question until they find someone who has chosen the same activity as them. Then, they sit down together. When everyone is sitting down, elicit what each group wants to do. Children answer and mime the activity. Then repeat the activity, asking children to circle another activity in a different color.

Unit 7   97

👁 Look. 👄 Say. ✨ Match.

Cross-curricular: Math

It's 6 o'clock.

It's 3 o'clock.

It's 11 o'clock.

It's 8 o'clock.

It's 1 o'clock.

Math: Telling the time. Point to the first clock. Ask: *What time is it?* and read the time aloud. Children repeat after you: *It's three o'clock.* Then point to the written times at the bottom of the page and say: *It's three o'clock. Can you find it?* Help children find the correct text. Children draw a line to match the clock to the written time. Continue with the other clocks and times, encouraging children to say the time as they match.

 Count. Color. Trace.

Numeracy

10 20 30 40 50 60 70 80

Numeracy: *eighty.* Point to the first column of soccer balls and ask: *How many balls can you see?* Count the balls in the first column (10), then say: *Let's count by tens.* Children count and answer, then color the balls in the last two columns and trace numbers 70 and 80. Finally, children practice counting by tens to eighty.

Unit 7

Say. Circle. Draw. Color. Review

What is a routine?

My favorite word in Unit 7 is:

_____

Unit 7

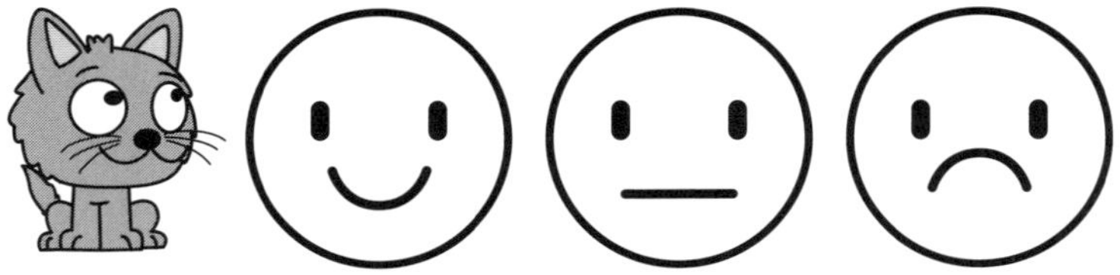

Vocabulary and Language Review: Ask the Big Question: *What is a routine?* Children look back through Unit 7 to recall what they have learned. Ask children to look at the 10 pictures from Unit 7. They say the words then circle the pictures that they are able to name. Then ask: *What is your favorite word in this unit?* Remind children of the words from the vocabulary lessons. Children write and draw a picture of their favorite word. If necessary, write the words on the board for children to copy. Children present their pictures to the class saying: *My favorite word is ...* . Answer the Big Question together, using their drawings and the pictures on the left as prompts. Finally, focus on the self-assessment activity. Ask: *How did you do in this unit?* Children color the face that shows how they feel they did.

How can we care for the Earth?

 Stick.  Match.  Say. Trace.

wood

paper

natural

rock

human-made

plastic

Vocabulary: *natural, human-made, wood, rock, paper, plastic.* Point to the first picture and say the word. Children point to the correct picture and repeat the word. Repeat with the other words. Say: *(Natural / Human-made). Stick (natural / human-made).* Children stick each sticker as you say it. Then point to the picture of the wood and ask: *Is it natural or human-made? (Natural.)* Children match the items to the correct adjective. They then point to each item saying: *(Wood) is (natural).* Finally, children trace the words. Children can color the objects in colors of their preference.

◯ Circle. ◡ Say.　　　　　　　　　　　　　　　Story

1 2 3 4

1 2 3 4

1 2 3 4

1 2 3 4

Language: *Is this picture (first) in the story? Which picture is (first)?* Look at the scenes from the story. Point to the first scene and ask: *Is this picture first in the story? (No.)* Ask: *Which picture is first?* Children point to the correct scene. They circle the number 1 under the scene to show that it is the first. Repeat with the second, third, and last scenes. Children then retell the story, using the scenes for reference.

 Say. Write.

Phonics

st sc

___atter

___evie

___hool

___and

Phonics: *Stevie, stand* /st/; *school, scatter* /sk/ (consonant blends). Point to the consonant blends in the box and read them aloud. Children repeat pointing to each consonant blend. Point to the first picture, read the gapped word below it and elicit the complete word *(scatter)*. Say the word again emphasizing the /sk/ sound and encourage children to point to the correct consonant blend in the box. Then, children write the letters to complete the word. Repeat with the other pictures and words. For *Stevie*, demonstrate how to write a capital 'S' on the board.

 Say. ✗ Cross. ✓ Mark. ✏ Color.

Literacy

1 Stevie waters the  .

2 Stevie feeds the  .

3 Stevie sees two 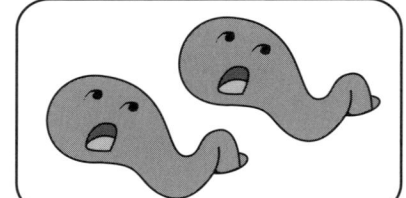 .

4 Stevie takes care of the  .

Do you like the story?

Literacy: Identifying a character's actions in a story. Point to the first picture and ask children what they see (a tree). Then point to the first sentence and read it aloud with children: *Stevie waters the ...* . Elicit *tree* as you point to the picture. Ask: *Is this correct?* (No.) Children put an X in the box next to the picture. Ask: *What does Stevie water in the story?* Elicit the correct answer. (*Plants at school / Flowers*.) Repeat with the other sentences. Children put an X next to the things Stevie doesn't do (he doesn't feed the butterflies and he doesn't see two worms) and a check mark next to the things he does do (he takes care of the yard). Finally, ask: *Do you like the story?* Children color the face that shows their opinion of the story.

 Color. Circle. Say.

Values

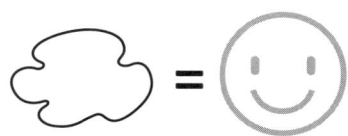 =  save water   ⬜ = ☹ waste water

Values: Saving water. Focus on each picture and ask: *What's he / she doing? Is he / she saving water?* For the pictures where the children are wasting water, discuss what they could do differently. Children choose two colors to represent *save water* and *waste water*, and complete the key at the top of the page. They then circle each picture in the correct color according to their key. They point to each picture and describe it: *(She)'s (wasting) water.*

 Say. Trace. Write.

Vocabulary

| glass   cardboard   soda |

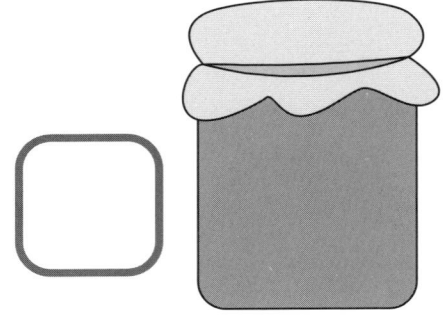

1 spoon

2 jar

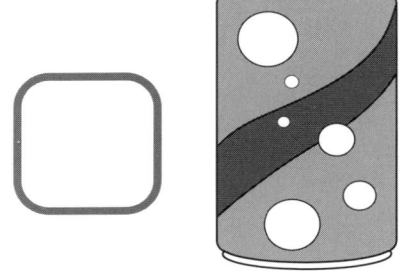

3 newspaper

4 s____ can

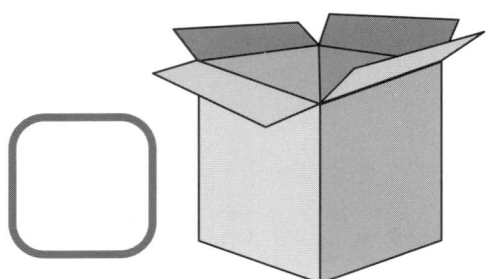

5 c_____ box

6 g____ bottle

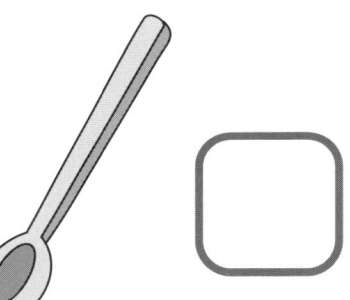

Vocabulary: *cardboard box, soda can, newspaper, spoon, jar, glass bottle.* Point to each picture and have children name the object. Repeat several times. Point to the first word and say: *One. Spoon.* Children repeat and trace the word. Say it again and have children find the corresponding picture and write the number 1 in the box. Repeat with the other words. For 4, 5, and 6, they also write the missing words, using the words in the box to help them.

Unit 8

Language: *What is it? It's a (soda can). Is it natural or human-made? I think it's (human-made).* Children look at the objects on the game board. Explain that some are natural and some are human-made. Tell them you are going to play a game where they need to listen and color, and that the objective is to get four colored objects in a row (across or down). Say: *Color something natural!* and children choose one item to color from anywhere in the game. Next say: *Color something human-made* and they do the same. Continue in this way, randomly choosing natural or human-made. When a child has colored four items in a row, they point to each and say *natural* or *human-made*.

Unit 8 107

 Count.  Draw. Write. Say.

Concept

2 + 4 = ___

5 + 2 = ___

3 + 6 = ___

1 + 9 = ___

Concept: Adding with a number line. Point to the first math problem and read it aloud: *Two plus four equals … .* Children count and draw the lines on the number line to arrive at the answer. They write the answer to complete the math problem. Finally, children say: *Two plus four equals six.* Repeat with the other math problems.

 Say.  Trace.  Write. Color.

Vocabulary

| plastic bag | garbage can | recycle | cloth bag |

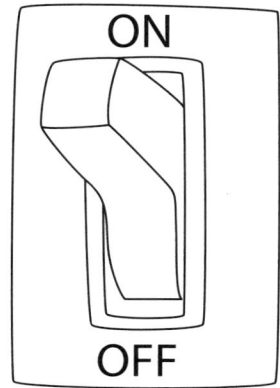

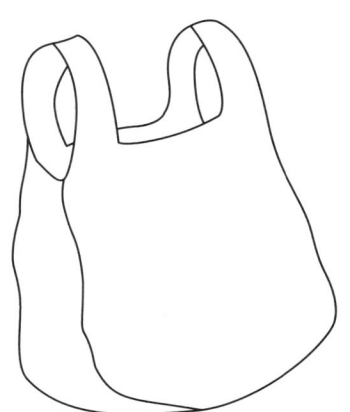

turn on   p_____   r_____

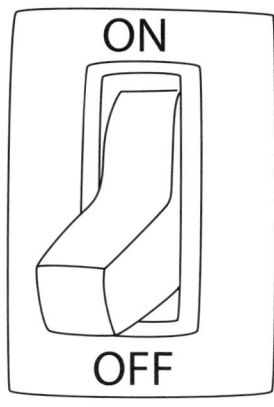

turn off   c_____   g_____

Vocabulary: *plastic bag, cloth bag, recycle, garbage can, turn on, turn off.* Point to each picture and have children name the object or action. Repeat several times. Then point to *turn on* and have children trace the word. Repeat with *turn off*. Then point to the first word in the box and say: *Plastic bag.* Children repeat and point to the correct picture. They trace the first letter, then write the rest of the word. Repeat with the other words in the box. Then point to each picture and ask: *Does this help the Earth?* Children color the pictures showing things that help the Earth.

✏️ Draw. ✏️ Write. ✨ Match. 😊 Say.

Language

| bottles   plastic   turn off   soda cans |

1 I recycle _____.

2 I _____ lights.

3 I don't use _____ bags.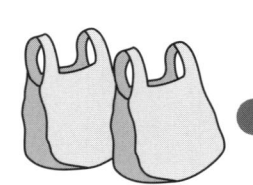

4 I don't put _____ in the garbage can.

Language: *What do you do to help the Earth? I (recycle soda cans). I don't (put bottles in the garbage can).* Children decorate the head on the right to look like themselves. Point to and read each word in the box. Children repeat, pointing to the word and the corresponding picture. Read the first sentence and point to the picture next to it. Children complete the sentence with the correct word from the box. Repeat with the other sentences. Children draw lines to match the things they do to the picture of themselves. Finally, children work in pairs and take turns asking and answering questions about the things they do to help the Earth: *What do you do to help the Earth? I (turn off lights).*

 **Look. Draw. Say.**

Speaking

What do you think about bees?

I think bees are beautiful.

Language: *What do you think about (bees)? I think (bees) are (beautiful). I think (pollution) is (terrible).* Point to Leo and read the question. Then point to the girl and read her answer. Children repeat. Then point to each picture and ask: *What do you think about (bees)?* Children think and draw a happy or a sad expression on the faces. Finally, repeat the question and invite children to give their opinions using the language: *I think (bees) are (beautiful).* Children can work in pairs, taking turns to ask and answer the questions.

Cross-curricular: Social Studies

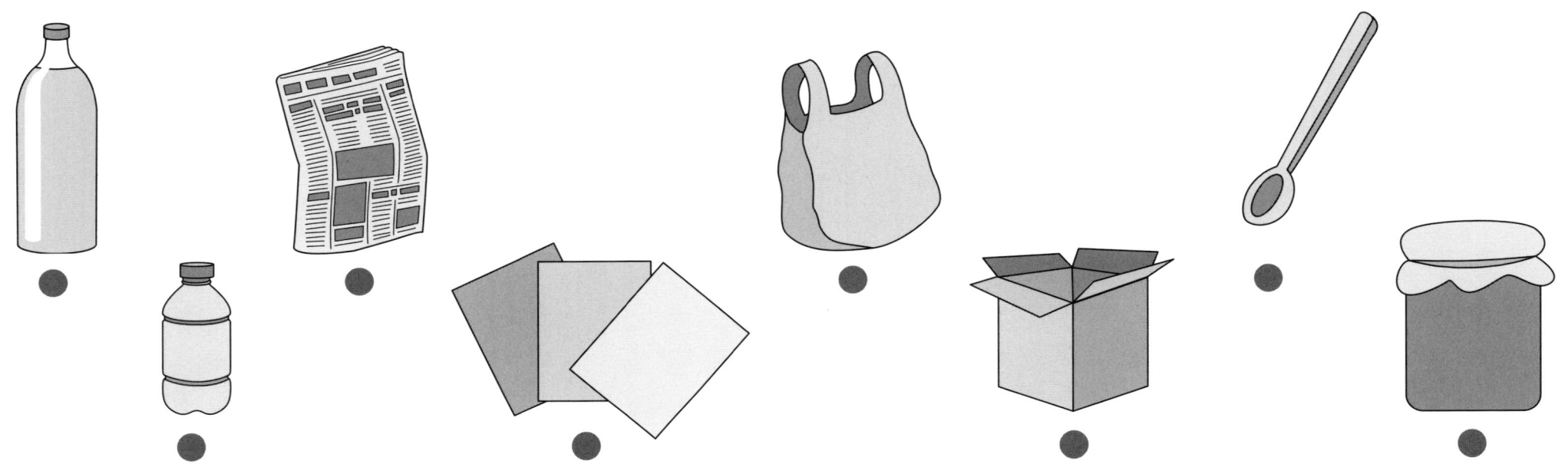

plastic

paper

glass

Social Studies: Identifying recyclable materials. Point to the recycling bins at the bottom of the page. Read aloud the label on the first bin, and children repeat. Ask: *What color are plastic recycling bins?* Children color the bin in the correct color. Repeat with the other bins. Alternatively, you can select together a different color for each bin. Then point to the glass bottle and ask: *What's this? Where does it go?* Children draw lines to match the items to the correct bin.

 Count. Color. Trace.

Numeracy

10 20 30 40 50 60 70 80 90

Numeracy: ninety. Point to the first column of soda cans and ask: *How many soda cans can you see?* Count the cans in the first column (10), then say: *Let's count by tens.* Children count and answer, then color the cans in the last two columns and trace numbers 80 and 90. Finally, children practice counting by tens to ninety.

Unit 8 113

Say. Circle. Draw. Color. Review

How can we care for the Earth?

My favorite word in Unit 8 is:

_____

Unit 8

 What do we do on vacation?

 Stick. Color. Say. Trace.

beach

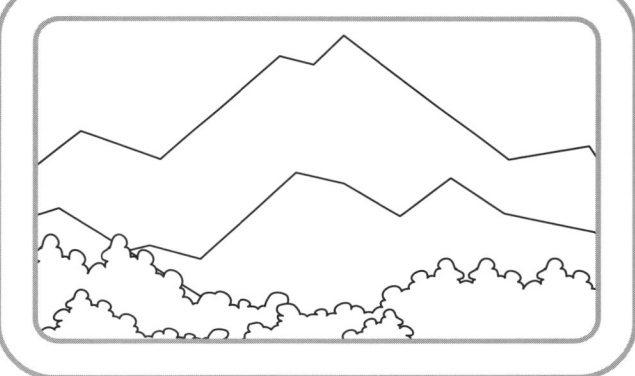
mountains

forest

amusement park

lake

summer camp

Language: *beach, mountains, forest, lake, amusement park, summer camp.* Point to the beach and say the word. Children point to the picture and repeat the word. Repeat with the other words. Say: *(Forest / Amusement park).* Stick the *(forest / amusement park).* Children stick each sticker as you say it. Then name the other places. Children point to each place as you say it. Children color the frame of their favorite place and they take turns to say its name. Finally, children trace the words. Children can color the places in colors of their preference.

✏️ Color. 😃 Say.

Story

Language: *Are they (happy)? happy, sad, tired, excited.* Look at the scenes from the story. Point to the four different types of emojis and elicit the feelings (happy, sad, tired, and excited). Then point to the first scene and ask: *How do they feel? Are they happy, sad or tired?* Children color the correct emoji. Repeat with the other scenes. Children then retell the story, using the scenes for reference.

 Say. Write. — Phonics

ng   sh   cl   ch   st

__ ine

__ ildren

si __

__ and

__ othes

Match. Draw. Say. Color.

Literacy

First · Next · Last

Do you like the story?

Literacy: Identifying the sequence of a story. Look at the words at the top of the page and read them aloud. Children repeat. Point to the first scene and ask: *Is this picture first in the story? (No.)* Ask: *Which picture is first?* Children point to the correct scene. They draw a line to match the word to the scene. Repeat with *next* and *last*. They draw the missing fire in the scene on the left. Children then retell the story, using the scenes for reference. Finally, ask: *Do you like the story?* Children color the face that shows their opinion of the story.

✓ **Mark.** ✏ **Color.** ◡ **Say.**

Values

Values: Relaxing and being calm. Focus on each picture and ask: *What's he / she doing? Is he / she relaxing?* Children put a check mark in the boxes next to the pictures that show someone relaxing and being calm. Then point to each picture again and ask: *Do you do this? How do you feel when you do this?* Children color the pictures that show things they do to relax. They then point to each picture and describe it.

Unit 9 119

Trace. Write. Talk. Mark.

Vocabulary

| sleeping bag | backpack |

cap			
towel			
sunglasses			
flashlight			
s _____			
b _____			

Vocabulary: *towel, flashlight, sleeping bag, sunglasses, cap, backpack.* Point to each picture and name the item. Children repeat. They trace the words for the first four items. Then point to and read the words in the box. Children repeat. They trace the first letter, then write the rest of each word next to the correct picture. Choose a confident child, and write their name at the top of the table. Ask: *Do you have a (cap)?* Record their answers with check marks or Xs. Children write their name at the top of the first column and complete it for themselves. They then work in pairs, taking turns to ask and answer and complete the next column for their partner. Repeat with different partners.

 **Draw.**  **Write.**  **Say.**

Language

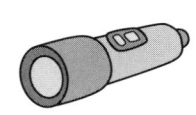

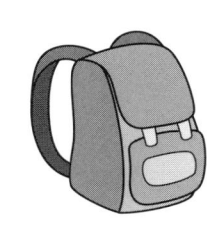

I take a _____ and a _____ to the beach.

Language: *What do you take to the beach? I take (a towel) to the beach. What else do you take to the beach?* Point to the items on the left and ask children to name them. Then focus on the empty suitcase and ask: *What do you take to the beach?* Then read the sentence at the bottom. Children repeat. Children draw what they want to take in their suitcase, and complete the sentences. They can look at the Student's Book page to help with spelling. Finally, they present their suitcases.

123 Count.  Draw.  Write. ⌣ Say. | Concept

4 − 2 = ____

1	2	3	4	5	6	7	8	9	10

8 − 5 = ____

1	2	3	4	5	6	7	8	9	10

10 − 8 = ____

1	2	3	4	5	6	7	8	9	10

7 − 6 = ____

1	2	3	4	5	6	7	8	9	10

Concept: *Taking away with a number line.* Point to the first math problem and read it aloud: *Four minus two equals ...* . Children count and draw the lines on the number line to arrive at the answer. They write the answer to complete the math problem. Finally, children say: *Four minus two equals two*. Repeat with the other math problems.

Point. Say. Trace. Write. **Vocabulary**

| hike   make a campfire   go on rides   ride a horse   row a boat   build a sandcastle |

b _ _ _ _ _

_ _ _ _ _ _ _ _ _

r _ _ _ _ _

_ _ _ _ _

g _ _ _ _

_ _ _ _ _

r _ _ _

_ _ _ _

h _ _ _

m _ _ _ _

Vocabulary: *build a sandcastle, hike, make a campfire, go on rides, row a boat, ride a horse.* Children point to the pictures and name each activity. Point to and read the words / phrases in the box at the top. Children repeat after you, pointing to each word / phrase as they say it. Point to the first picture on the left and elicit the activity. Children trace the first letter, then write the rest of the phrase. Repeat with the other pictures. Children work in pairs, taking turns to point to an activity for their partner to name.

Look. Write. Say.

Language

> mountains   beach   forest

1 She builds sandcastles at the _____.

2 She rides a horse in the _____.

3 She hikes in the _____.

 Look. Color. Say. — Speaking

 Where are you going on vacation?

 I'm going to a lake.

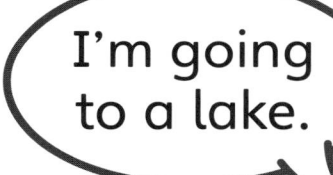

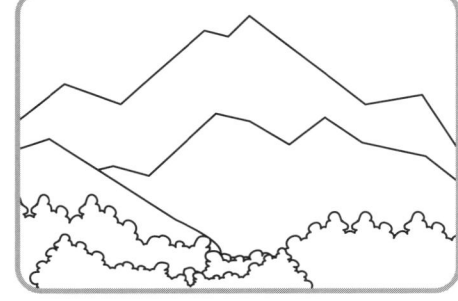
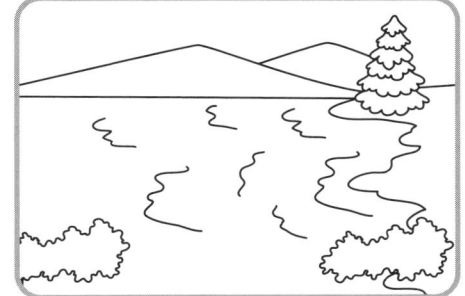

Language: *Where are you going on vacation? I'm going to (the beach). What are you going to do (at the beach)? I'm going to (build a sandcastle).* Point to the question and answer in the speech bubbles and read them aloud. Children repeat. Children choose one of the places on the left to go to, and color the picture. Then focus on the activities on the right of the page and elicit the words. Ask: *What are you going to do (at the beach)?* Children choose two or three activities and color them. Ask the questions again and elicit answers from several children. Children ask and answer the questions in pairs.

Unit 9 125

👆 **Point.** ✨ **Match.** ⭕ **Circle.** ✏️ **Write.**

Cross-curricular: Art

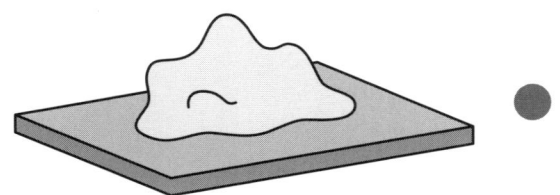

 stones

 clay

leaves

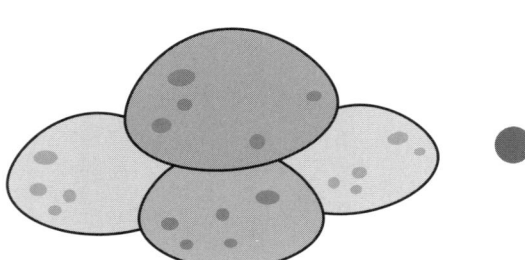

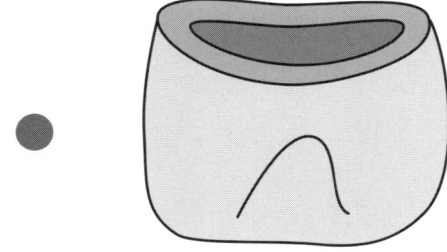

I can make art with _____.

 Count. Color. Trace.

Numeracy

10 20 30 40 50 60 70 80 90 100

Numeracy: one hundred. Point to the first column of caps and ask: *How many caps can you see?* Count the caps in the first column (10), then say: *Let's count by tens.* Children count and answer, then color the caps in the last two columns and trace numbers 90 and 100. Finally, children practice counting by tens to one hundred.

Unit 9 127

Say. Circle. Draw. Color.

What do we do on vacation?

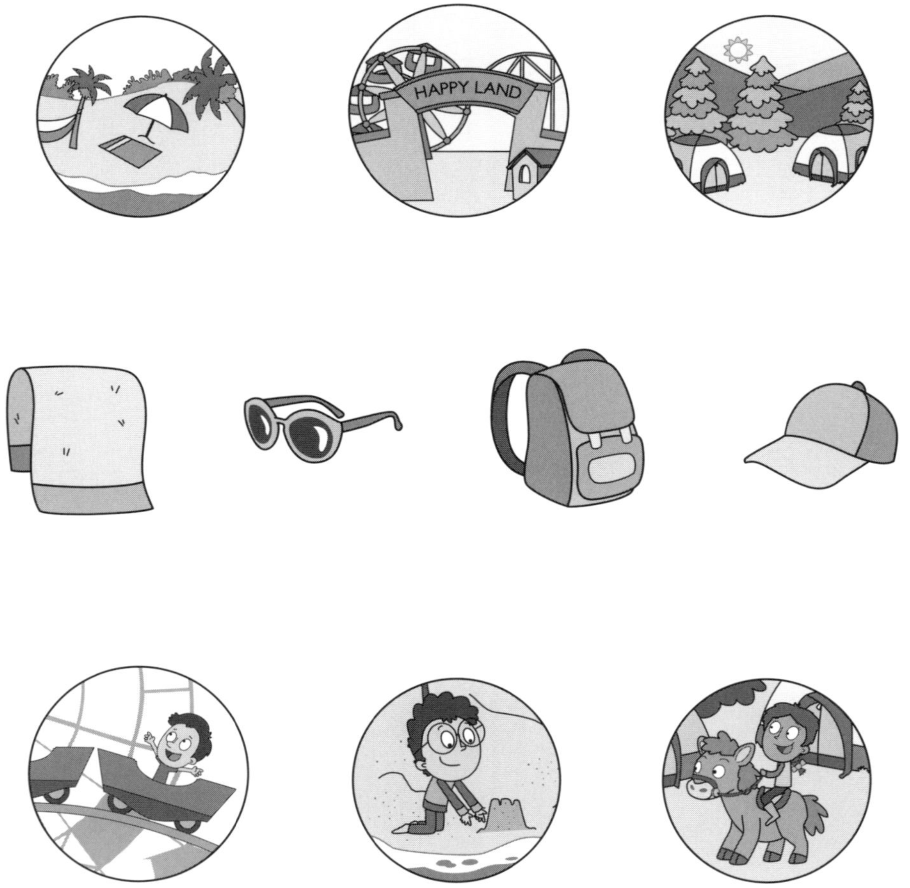

My favorite word in Unit 9 is:

____

Unit 9

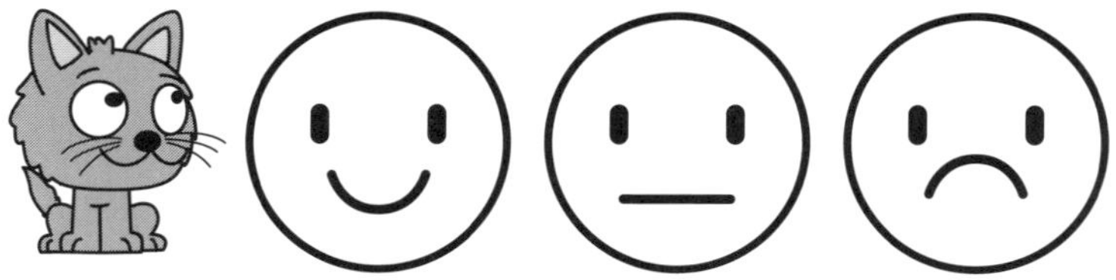

Vocabulary and Language Review: Ask the Big Question: *What do we do on vacation?* Children look back through Unit 9 to recall what they have learned. Ask children to look at the 10 pictures from Unit 9. They say the words then circle the pictures that they are able to name. Then ask: *What is your favorite word in this unit?* Remind children of the words from the vocabulary lessons. Children write and draw a picture of their favorite word. If necessary, write the words on the board for children to copy. Children present their pictures to the class saying: *My favorite word is … .* Answer the Big Question together, using their drawings and the pictures on the left as prompts. Finally, focus on the self-assessment activity. Ask: *How did you do in this unit?* Children color the face that shows how they feel they did.

Picture Dictionary

Children open the book to the corresponding unit. They point to a picture and name it. If children cannot name the vocabulary item, say the word and have them repeat it. Finally, children color the pictures. You can use the Picture Dictionary to review vocabulary throughout the year.

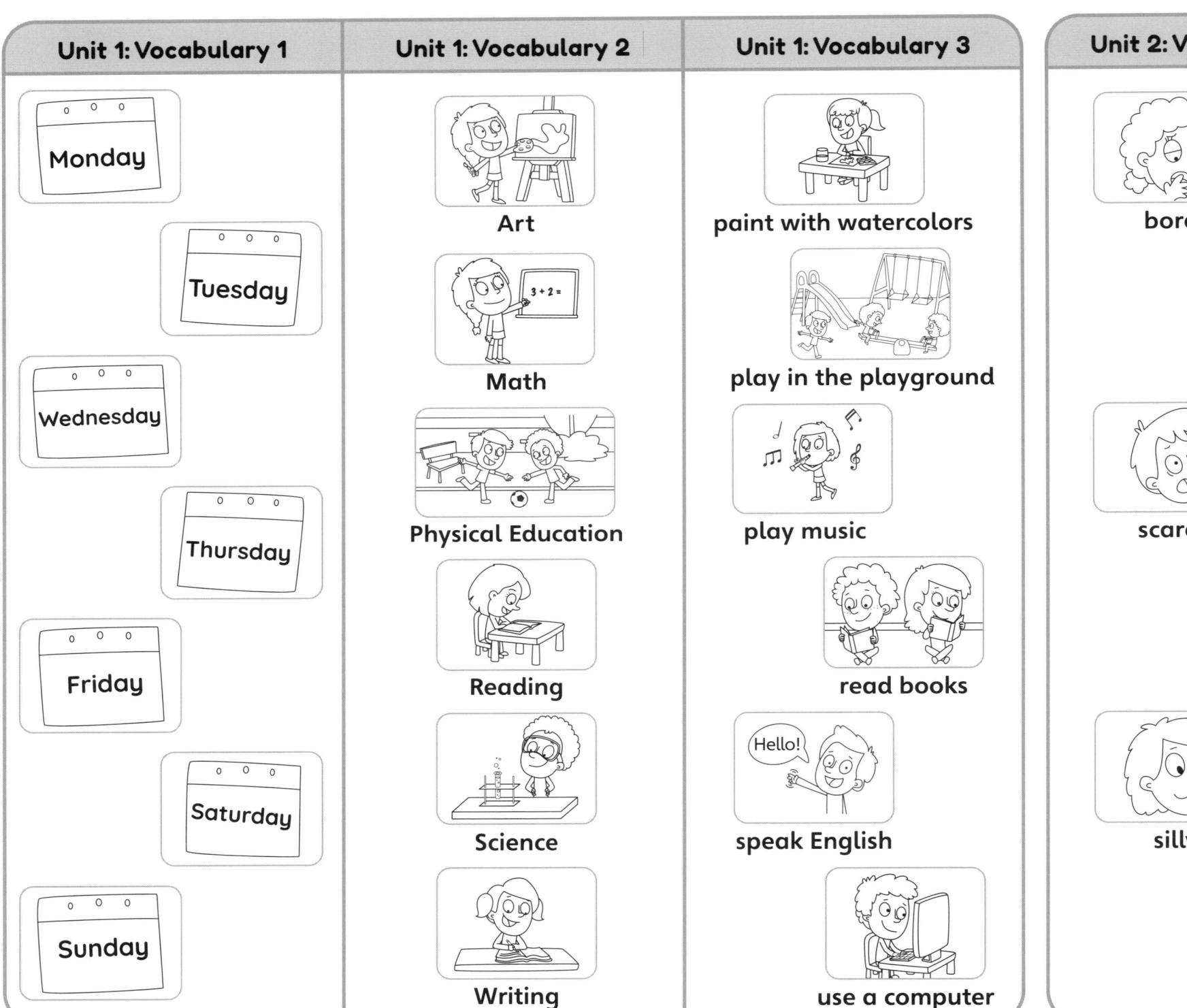

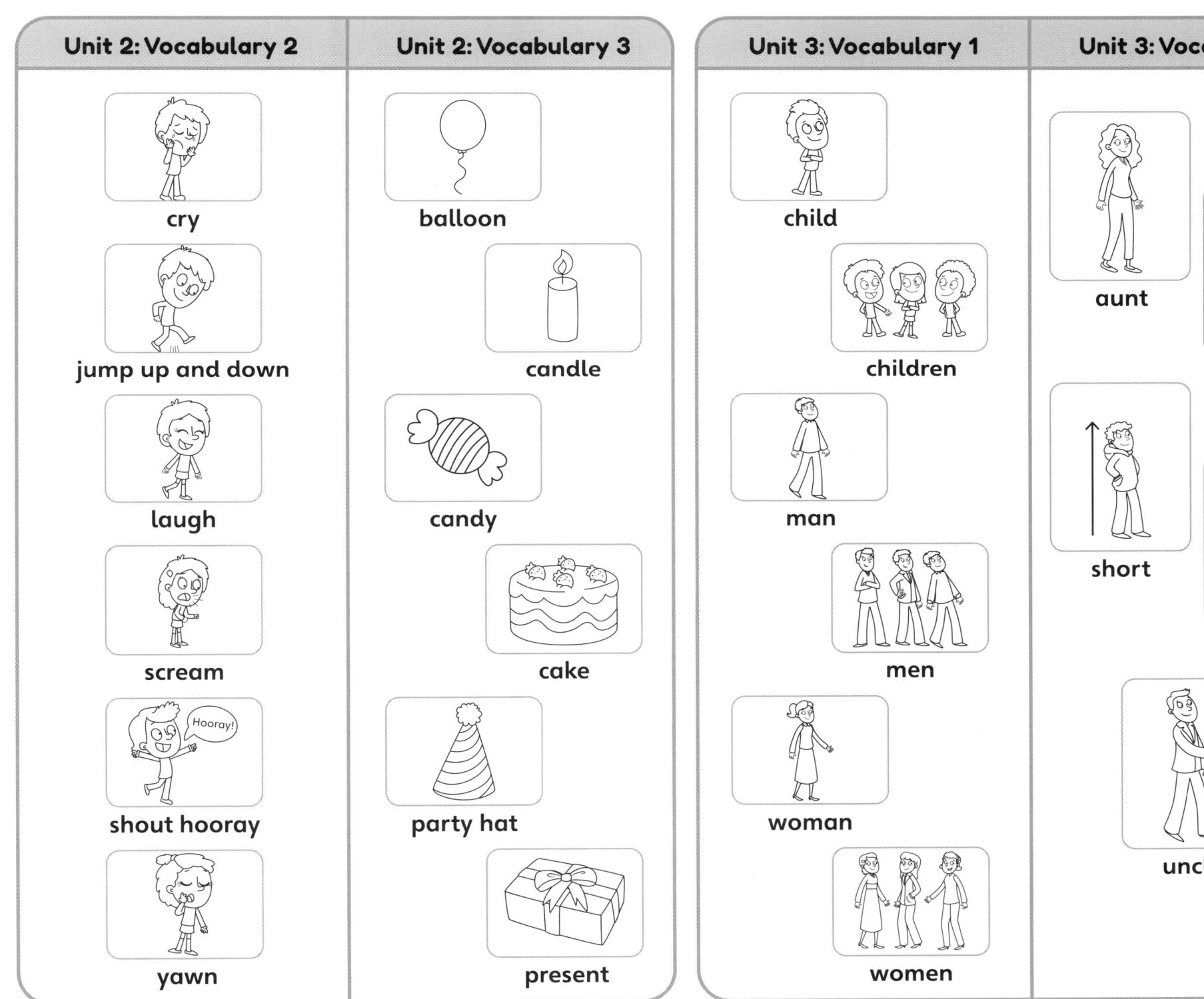

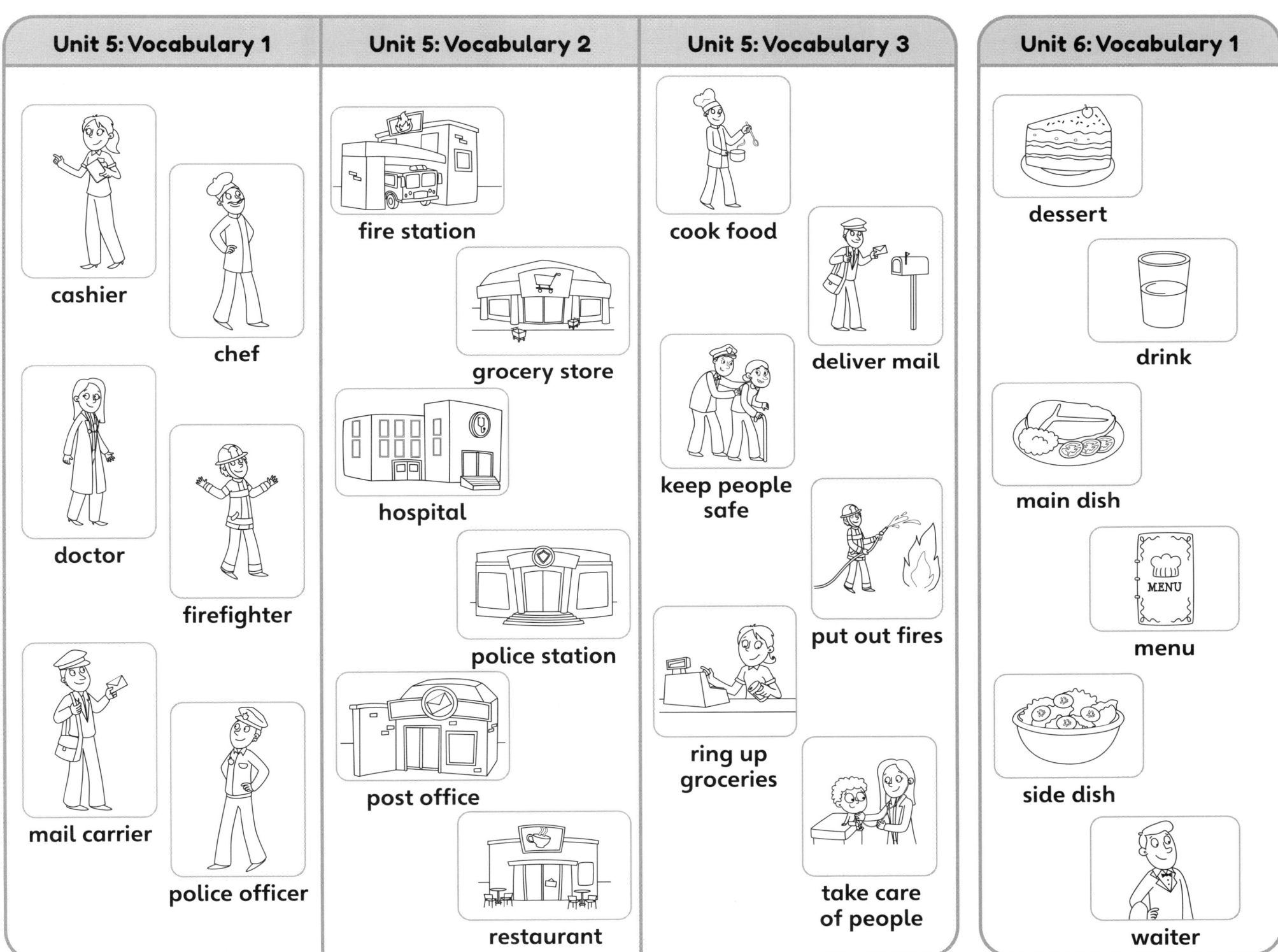

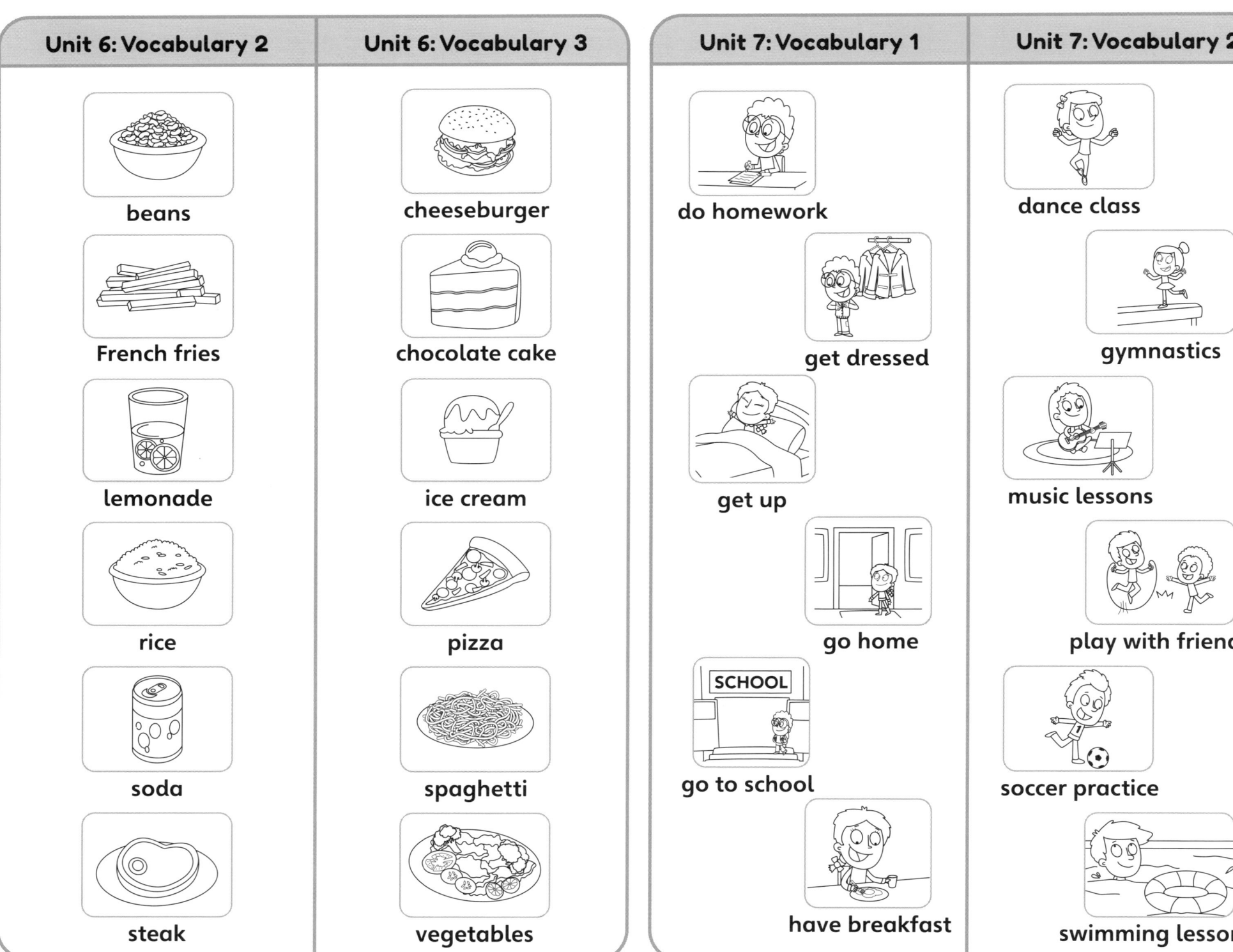

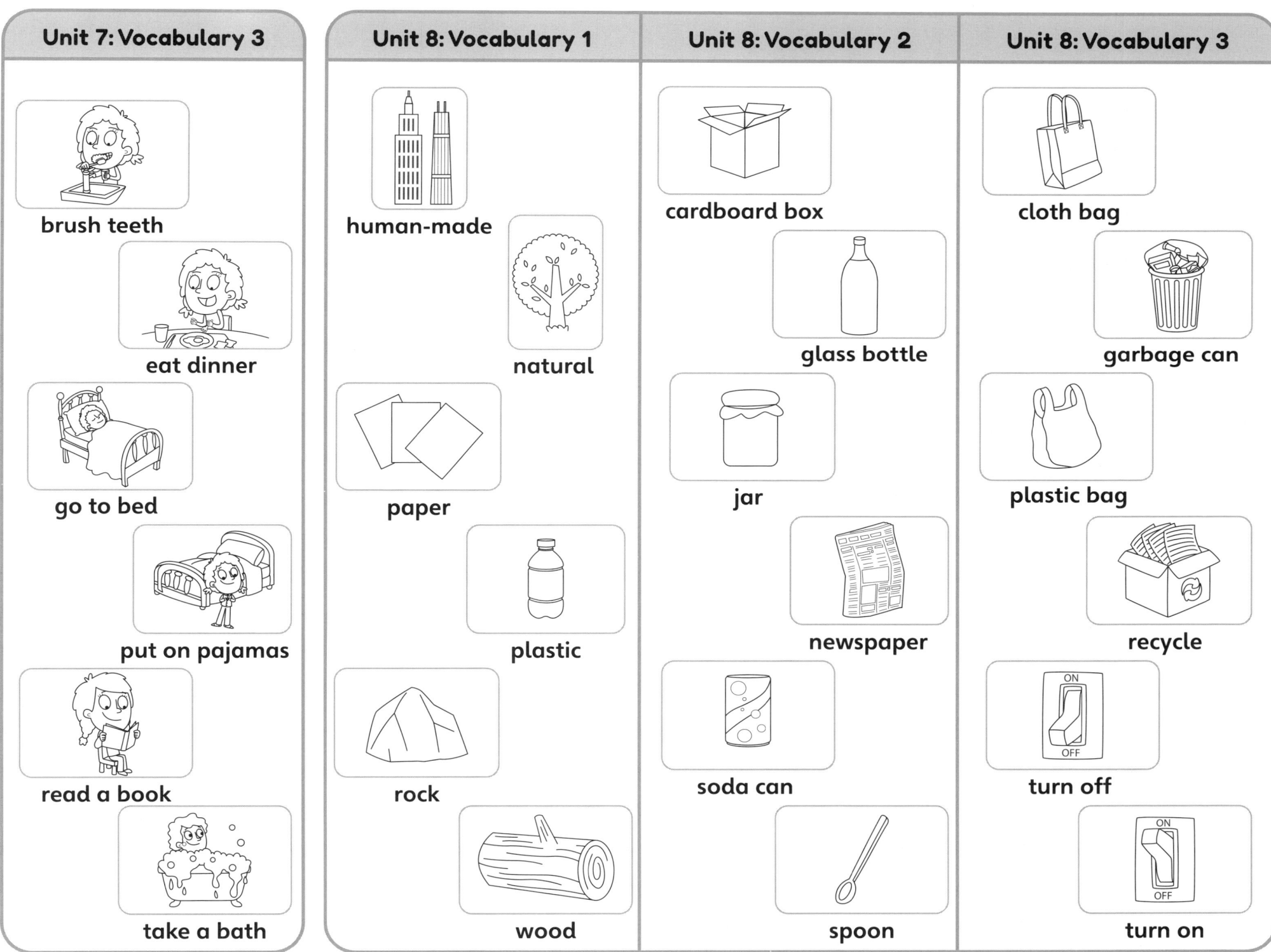

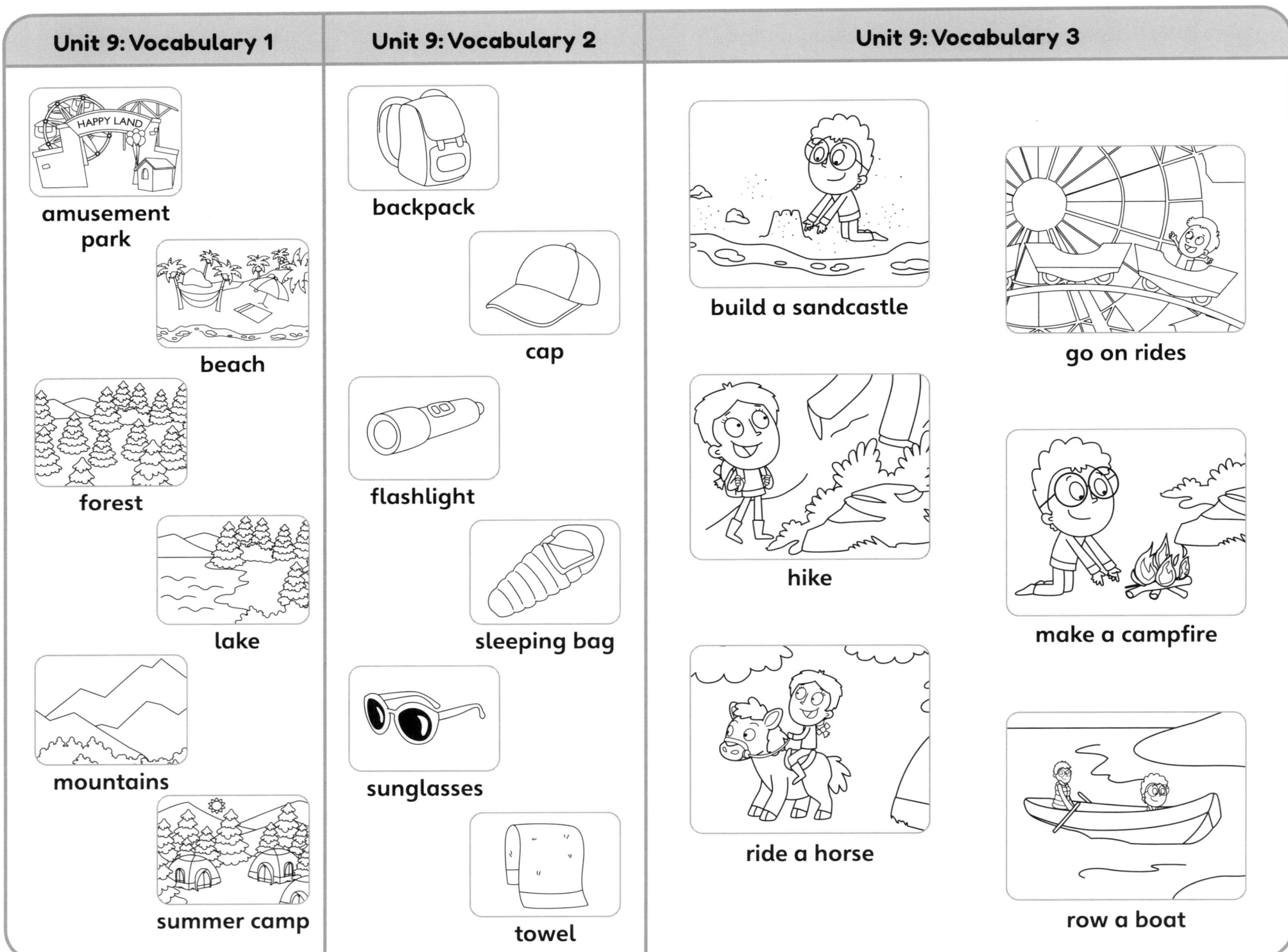

Unit 1, p. 3

Unit 2, p. 17

Unit 3, p. 31

Unit 5, p. 59

Unit 4, p. 45

Unit 6, p. 73

Unit 7, p. 87

Unit 9, p. 115

Unit 8, p. 101